Heart AND Sold

Heart AND Sold

How to Survive and Build a Recession-Proof Business

VALERIE FITZGERALD

ATRIA PAPERBACK

New York London Toronto Sydney

ATRIA PAPERBACK

A Division of Simon & Schuster, Inc.
1230 Avenue of the Americas
New York, NY 10020

First Atria Paperback edition May 2009

ATRIA PAPERBACK and colophon are trademarks
of Simon & Schuster, Inc.

For information about special discounts for bulk purchases,
please contact Simon & Schuster Special Sales at
1-866-506-1949 or business@simonandschuster.com.

The Simon & Schuster Speakers Bureau can bring authors to your
live event. For more information or to book an event contact the
Simon & Schuster Speakers Bureau at 1-866-248-3049 or visit our
website at www.simonspeakers.com.

"After a While" (poem) © 1971 by Veronica A. Shoffstall. Reprinted
with permission.

Designed by Jaime Putorti

Manufactured in the United States of America

10 9 8 7 6 5 4 3 2 1

Library of Congress Cataloging-in-Publication Data

Fitzgerald, Valerie.
  Heart and sold / How to survive and build a recession-proof
business / Valerie Fitzgerald.
    p. cm.
  1. Real estate agents. 2. Real estate business. 3. Success in
business. 4. Fitzgerald, Valerie. I. Title.

HD1382.F58 2008
333.33068—dc22   2008004807

ISBN-13: 978-1-4165-4292-6
ISBN-10:   1-4165-4292-2
ISBN-13: 978-1-4391-6399-3 (ebook)

To my daughter Vanessa, my miracle baby.

Having you changed me in ways you will never

know. You have always been a beacon of light

through the darkness for me.

I love being your mother.

AFTER A WHILE

After a while, you learn the subtle difference
Between holding a hand and chaining a soul
And you learn that love doesn't mean leaning
And company doesn't mean security,
And you begin to learn that kisses aren't contracts
And presents aren't promises,
And you begin to accept your defeats
With your head up and your eyes open
With the grace of a woman, not the grief of a child,
And you learn to build all your roads on today
Because tomorrow's ground is too uncertain for plans
And futures have a way of falling down in mid-flight.
After a while, you learn
Even sunshine burns if you get too much
So you plant your own garden and decorate your own soul,
Instead of waiting for someone to bring you flowers.
And you learn that you really can endure ...
That you really are strong,
And you really do have worth.
And you learn and you learn
With every goodbye, you learn ...

—VERONICA A. SHOFFSTALL

Contents

Contents

Author's Note

Writing a book and having it published take longer than I would have ever imagined. When I was approached to write my story of triumph over adversity, the U.S. economy was strong and showed few signs of wavering. Three years later, we are faced with a different story. During times like these, we question our financial choices, both personal and professional. However, it is important to remember that we are going through a cycle, and this too shall pass.

America's story is written by people who have reinvented themselves after encountering adversity and facing it head on. I urge you to walk away from financial fears, to persevere through your challenges, and to grab hold of the life you desire most. I have reinvented my life many times and have learned that regardless of economic upset, a business foundation needs to be strong. Use the tools in these pages to build a strong foundation for *your* business. If you have an existing business, make sure you go back and reinforce your foundation with the strategies I share with you. While confirming the strength of your foundation, you will reinforce the spirit you have in your heart to master any cycle—any market—and succeed.

This book will show you how I overcame tremendous personal and financial adversities to create a life that is both sustainable and rewarding, no matter what the outside circumstances. I know you can do the same.

Introduction

In many ways I am like you. I have had my share of lessons learned, both good and bad. It goes with the territory of being an adult. Just as there is no blueprint for how to be a parent, there is no blueprint for how to be an adult and take control of your destiny. The most important lessons we learn in life are through trial and error. The consequences of our choices become our guiding path to betterment, to being better mothers, better fathers, better providers. It's been my experience that we "bump into our lives." I know I have.

This book is my personal story which I hope will take you on a journey of your own personal discoveries. There are things that you may relate to or that may ring your inner bell. When they do, I hope that you will take a few minutes for yourself and reflect on what these discoveries can mean for your life.

I am sharing my life and stories through this book to open up doors to new possibilities for you. As you will see, there are very few mistakes I *didn't* make, yet I worked through all of them and built an incredible life for myself and my daughter.

So give up the excuses you have been living uncomfortably with. Throw the doors open to success!

Heart AND Sold

There is in every true woman's heart a spark of heavenly fire, which lies dormant in the broad daylight of prosperity; but which kindles up and beams and blazes in the dark hour of adversity.

—WASHINGTON IRVING

CHAPTER ONE

My Story: The Will to Survive

The room was plain and sparsely furnished. A borrowed couch, a small bed, and a crib sat forlornly on the bland beige carpet. A blond woman sat quietly, her thin back poised against the borrowed couch while her three-month-old daughter kicked and squirmed on the floor beside her. This woman had fled New York to start a new life in California. Her apartment in New York City had been sublet for two years. She had left behind a violent ex-husband, her luxurious belongings, and her former life as a model. On the floor of her closet behind a box of diapers was a wrinkled leather bag containing all the money she had in the world, raised by selling the jewelry she had acquired during her modeling days. She had no skills outside modeling, no higher education, no backup plan. She was a woman of a certain age and wasn't a valuable commodity in the fashion business anymore, and the prince on the white horse who was going to save her had ridden off long ago. She was alone. She was poor. She was afraid. She picked up her daughter and held her close to her heart. She closed her eyes and inhaled the wonderful scent of baby powder, baby clothes, and the delicious baby smell every mother recognizes instantly. It calmed the woman's fears. She looked down into her baby's clear, wide blue eyes. "I'm not going to fail you," she said. "I don't know how, I don't know what I'm going to do, but I'll figure something out. I'll make a good life for us. I promise."

Today that same woman is an entrepreneur, a philanthropist, and a corporate executive. This was not by chance or coincidence. It was because of determination, the drive to overcome, and just plain hard work. I know a lot about that woman, because that woman who made the promise to her tiny daughter is me, Valerie Fitzgerald.

In the beginning of this journey, it never occurred to me that my life would be inspirational to anyone else. It really wasn't so much that I had the desire to be successful— I *had to be* successful. There was no other choice for me. But back then, I was consumed with thoughts about how I was going to pay my bills and make a great life for my daughter. So you can only imagine that when I hear the words "entrepreneur," "philanthropist," and "corporate executive," there is still a part of me that says, "Who? Where?"

I look around the room and am surprised that they are talking about me. When I was approached about writing a book about my life, I was a little nervous. I think I made every mistake it was possible that a woman could make with men, with money, and with friends. If there was a bad choice to be made, I made it. If there was a bad investment, I put money into it. If there was a bad guy lurking in the shadows, I ran up and introduced myself.

It's just the way I am, or at least it was the way I was. It's not that I was dumb, but I was young and naive. I was also inexperienced. I was a little girl born in South Dakota whose parents left for the bright lights of Hollywood. When I was fifteen, I got my first modeling job. I had taken Polaroids of myself and wearing my Sunday best dropped them off at *Teen* magazine. That first experience in modeling ended up with me being on the cover three times. I was so excited to have a career! When I was in my late teens, one of the friends I met modeling told me all about New York, her boyfriend, and the fantastic people she'd met there. To the ears of a nineteen-year-old it sounded like heaven. So off I went to New York and my friend's studio apartment on the Upper East Side.

Imagine a young girl with forty dollars in her pocket, a few modeling pictures, and some clothes landing in New York amidst skyscrapers and taxis blaring their horns in the constant noise that can only be described as the music of New York City. When I arrived at Maggie's place, my new home, I was in for a shock. The room could barely be called an apartment. It had no closets or kitchen, just a hotplate and a small refrigerator next to the bathtub. Glamorous? Exciting? More like horrifying! I walked around the place, which took about fifteen seconds, and I realized there was no bed. Where was I to sleep? Was this a joke? It took me about twenty minutes to realize the room came with a Murphy bed—the kind that pulls out of the wall. Well here I was in the glamorous city of New York in my own "place."

It's not that I was ungrateful. I was so thankful to my friend for subletting her apartment, but the whole experience was foreign to me. No matter what, I was happy to have a place to stay, but the rent was steep—I had to pay Maggie six hundred dollars each month. Since I only had forty dollars in my pocket, somehow I needed to figure out right away how I was going to come up with the money for living expenses and another five hundred and sixty dollars. Mind you, this was New York in the 1970s, and six hundred dollars was a fortune to me—especially when I didn't have a job. I took my portfolio and pounded the streets.

There was no Wall Street look for me in those days. I was a California girl—blond hair straight down to my waist, cork platform shoes, and a dress . . . well, a dress that could only be described today as a muumuu. There I was, calling modeling agencies straight out of the phone book. With every call I made, I knew I couldn't keep letting them hang up on me. I had to find something to say that would get their attention—something that would get my foot in the door.

There was no way I was going to fail based on a phone call. So I dialed the next number and said, "Hi, I'm Valerie Fitzgerald, and I'm in New York only for a few days. I'm from California"—which I knew might make them hang up on me. "I'm the Coppertone Girl and . . ." The names of other campaigns I had done flew out of my mouth.

I had to get an appointment, and not one three months later, from those phone calls. I charmed, laughed, joked with everyone on the phone. Since I didn't physically look like a New York model with my waist-length hair, I was slightly nervous about what they might think when they met me, but I didn't give up. By the end of the day I ended up with appointments to see three of the top modeling agencies in New York.

I remember vividly my first few days in the city. It was early September, and the heavy air stirred as a cool breeze with the hint of fall swept by. People poured around me as I strolled down the streets. The pungent smell of hot dogs and roasted nuts washed over me. I felt so small. The lights of the tall buildings glittered overhead like watchful guardians of my fate. I was hypnotized by how fast everyone and everything was moving.

After several days of taking subways and often-missed buses to meet modeling agents, one in particular made me feel as though she believed in me. It was Eileen Ford at the Ford Modeling Agency. I clearly recall going into their offices on Fifty-eighth Street and First Avenue. It was a small brownstone building. At the time, the Ford Agency was the most prestigious in the world, and Eileen Ford was to be feared.

I walked up the steps to the small reception area, where there were at least thirty girls waiting to meet their fate. I was scared but not deterred. To be there, we all had to believe we had "something" the Ford Agency would want—and soon we would find out if we really did have it. Modeling agencies are very busy places. They have a million phones ringing at the same time, and when you meet the agents you are never quite sure if they will ever remember your name once you leave.

Well, I did end up signing with the Ford Modeling Agency and will forever be thankful to them for their guidance and the opportunities they presented to me. Unlike on the streets of New York, where people would stop and look at me, in the modeling world I was nothing exceptional. Everything from my head to my toes was scrutinized by the agents. One day after I signed the contract to be represented by Ford, one of their senior agents said to me that I was just one more girl from California with hair to my waist. So what made me so special? This person threw me off track so badly that she made me question my self-worth, and all I could do about it was go to my studio apartment, pull down my Murphy bed, and cry. It seemed like a long cry, but this girl from California wasn't going to let anyone get to her. So I got up—my bed sprang to the wall like a salute—and off I went for a walk down Second Avenue in my muumuu.

It was around this time that I met a guy named Joe. Joe is not his real name, but the story is true. I met him at a cocktail party, and I distinctly remember having an ache in my body when I looked at him. Not a good ache, mind you, but a visceral response that was alarming and a bit frightening.

Remember what I said earlier about the girl who held her hand out to the bad guy? That was me! The whole night was so surreal when I think back to it. Here was this man, clearly powerful and in control. I was curious about the small group of people who had gathered around him. I did not join the group. I felt more comfortable standing on the other side of the room, chatting and laughing with my friends, but all the time watching him. His energy was magnetizing.

The men listened attentively, eyebrows furrowed. Women swayed in anticipation of what he would say next. Eventually they all erupted in laughter at something he said. A friend of mine who knew the man offered to introduce him to me, but I declined. I was still feeling a bit weird about the whole thing.

"Oh you have to meet him!" she gushed. "He's great! He's charming and he would totally take care of you." She winked and I plastered a fake smile on my face. My body was wiser than her words. I felt uncomfortable, yet fascinated—almost like the way you feel when you see a car accident. You know it is most likely a bad situation, but you look anyway.

I had such a strange response when I was introduced to him that I excused myself to go to the ladies room because the feeling was so odd, so foreign. Today, I recognize that feeling as a warning. But, at that time, naive Valerie was curious. Joe pursued me for about a year. After our initial meeting, he had taken an obvious interest in me and would often call to invite me to exciting things he was doing. After every date, he would send me flowers. It began to feel good, and I enjoyed his attention.

Meanwhile, rain or shine, I rode my bike to go-sees with my modeling portfolio strapped to my back. Many times when I parked my bike, I would have to detach the front tire and take it with me along with my portfolio to the photographer's studio. Otherwise, the bike would likely not be there when I returned.

One day, while I was riding my bicycle to one of my shoots, a taxi sideswiped me. I skinned my knee and scraped my palm but was otherwise unhurt. Unfortunately, I could not say the same about my bike. It was destroyed.

When Joe found out, he gallantly offered the services of his limousine. It was a little awkward at first. I didn't want to accept anything from him, but he persisted. I was nervous, but not foolish. Who on earth could turn down the services of a limousine from a handsome rich man who persistently pursued her? His car was thrilling and handy, but a bit pretentious for transportation to a modeling shoot that paid only a hundred dollars. So when I used his car, I had the driver drop me off a block away, like a kid embarrassed by her parents at school. There were times I would have this car drop me off at the subway. I admit, I wasn't strong enough to say no to this powerful man. I came up with every excuse in the book not to have dinner with Joe until I finally broke down and agreed. From that dinner on, it was like getting on a roller coaster of luxury. He showered me with gifts: fantastic designer clothes, trips I could only have dreamed of before, and rides in his helicopter.

Despite my earlier feelings, I thought I had finally found my prince. I was totally overwhelmed. No one had ever shown this kind of interest in me. No one had ever been so generous with me. No one could be this wonderful. Joe became my world. I began laughing at his stories. I had stepped from one world into a fairy tale. I was Cinderella. I swallowed that nagging feeling of fear with glasses of expensive white wine. The gifts and trips he gave me silenced that part of my mind. I was in love. I was in love with him, with his life, and with his things. He was everything to me. As my life with Joe unfolded, I was paraded here and presented there. Every single day I experienced amazing things I never had dreamed about as a girl from South Dakota.

You would think I would be excited and energized by all this. You would think I would be on top of the world. I wasn't. I felt smaller and smaller, dwarfed by this lavish lifestyle. I ate dinner in places where the prices made my head reel. I went to parties where the chandelier alone could buy my childhood home ten times over. I listened to Wall Street power brokers spar, each man attempting to trump the last statement made.

While on one of our exotic trips to Haiti, Joe proposed to me out of the blue. We married the next day. At the time, it felt so right to be with this man. But eventually I began to see my life for what it was. I was a prop. I was a toy. I was the beautiful service platter that completed the set of Joe's dishes. That was me. Beautiful trophy wife. Only I didn't fully understand my role then. I remember one time when we were having dinner with friends at a very exclusive restaurant in New York. I was eager to get involved in the conversation, which revolved around the men and their business dealings. I was tired of sitting like the other wives and girlfriends in admiring silence beside their man. I thought I would just dive in with a question, to open up the conversation to all of us. "Gee, isn't it interesting that the Wall Street market is experiencing a steady climb to profit," I said.

I knew this to be true because I had read it in *Time* magazine. I was feeling excited to participate in the evening. I was sure this would impress the men, involve the women, and make my husband proud. There was silence. Ed, one of the men at the table, started laughing. One by one the other men began to laugh. The women just gaped at me in horror. Joe reached over and patted my hand. "That's adorable, honey, now shut up and let the men talk." I was humiliated. At that moment, I could have dropped through the floor from embarrassment. Not one woman uttered a word of support. Not one man defended me. The silence was deafening.

I felt dizzy and sick at the same time. The annoying voice of self-doubt, which I call the "monkey on my shoulder," began screeching. "You did it this time! Too bad you're worthless. Just shut up, smile, and look pretty." I never again opened my mouth at that dinner or any other dinner with my husband. It was more than just my words that fell silent. There was a part of me that went into hibernation that day. I won't say it died, because it was still there. It was just buried under layers of hurt and humiliation. My marriage to Joe continued, a predictable whirlwind of status. I withdrew more and more into myself, becoming a person I hardly recognized. I was beautiful and silent, like a statue. The only time I felt like my old self was when I was away from my husband. But even that was to change.

One night, I came home from a modeling job. My husband was angry. I had never seen him lose his temper before. His face burned scarlet and his eyes glittered like bright angry chips of steel. His body was stiff with rage, coiled tightly as he paced the floor with eerily measured steps. I was scared. I didn't know what had happened to make him this angry. I wasn't privy to any of his thoughts, his fears, his stresses, or his work. Without warning his knotted fist struck my face. My eye exploded in pain, and I fell to the ground. All I could think of was how to get away. I wanted to run, but all I could do was cower in fear and drag myself away to the farthest corner of our closet. I hid under the hanging clothes, sobs erupting from my chest in great waves, choking and crippling me. I pulled my legs tightly into my chest, crying until I couldn't cry anymore.

There was nothing left of me. My fairy-tale husband and life had shattered on the marble floor like a fallen mirror— the razor-sharp shards of glass lacerating my hopes, my dreams, and my heart. The next day he sent me roses with a diamond bracelet dangling off one stem. To him it was his way of saying I'm sorry. Little did I know, it was a handcuff hiding amid a floral bouquet. The next day, and for many days after that, I told the Ford Modeling Agency I was sick. I couldn't show up to work with bruises on my face. My face was my currency; without it, I was of no value to them, let alone to myself. But I had fallen in love with Joe. He was my husband. I was supposed to stay with him for better or worse. I had had the better. Now I was experiencing the worse. But it got worse, far worse. In my unsophisticated and inexperienced view of life, I was sure our marriage would improve. We were even talking about having children, even though I had been told many times by doctors that I would probably never be able to conceive.

At one point in our tumultuous relationship, I must admit that I wasn't sure I wanted to have children with Joe. When I told him how I felt, he exploded. The face that I had known to be red with anger became purple with rage. I ran to the bathroom and locked myself inside, but he broke through the door easily. He threw me to the floor, sat on my chest, and pounded my face. I was bleeding so badly, he took me to the hospital, where he dumped me in the parking lot and drove away. I crawled on my hands and knees into the emergency room. My eyes were swollen shut. I had a concussion and a fractured jaw.

I remember a woman in the hospital pressing a piece of paper into my hand. On it was a phone number—a help line for battered women. That was the first time I ever thought of myself as a battered women.

Through all the physical abuse, I never thought of myself that way. In those days, you did not talk about what was happening in your marriage, much less that your husband hit you. First, there was nothing anyone could do about it. And second, the first question from most people was, "Well, what did you do to deserve it?" No woman deserves to be hit, and fortunately today there are both better public awareness and agencies to assist battered women.

Today, charges can be pressed against the abuser based on injuries alone, but in those days, the police needed my consent. Being a good little wife, and a broken woman, I refused to press charges against my husband. I wanted him arrested for what he did to me, but I was afraid of what he would do. So I did nothing.

After I was released from the hospital, I went to stay with friends. The secret was out and I felt ashamed. My self-esteem was a shambles, and my face was not much better. My mind was spinning with a million questions. Where am I going to live? What if he comes after me? Will my face return to normal so I can work? What am I going to do? He has everything. While I did make some money in modeling, I had put everything into our joint account. Joe said he was investing it for me. I had never seen this account, although I inquired many times. When I tried to return home to pick up my personal possessions I discovered that he had changed the locks. He had closed our joint bank account and canceled all our credit cards. Because I was leaving him, I was walking away with nothing but my freedom. After several years of bitter divorce negotiations I received a nominal amount of money, which could never replace everything I had left. However, there is no gem, no coin, no fur that could ever take my freedom again. I was no longer naive. I was no longer unsophisticated.

I was no longer the open-hearted, fairy-tale-believing young girl who had handed over her money, her life, and her heart. I would never again be seduced by a man's wealth, power, or influence into selling my soul. I would never again ignore the warning signs I felt that day when we first met. I would get back on my own feet and live on my own terms. No one would ever leave me homeless and penniless again. I was never going to give away my power like I did with Joe.

It took time for my face to heal, but it did. It took a lot longer for my heart to heal. Modeling was all I knew how to do, and my husband had kept and probably destroyed my modeling portfolio. That book of photos was what landed me work, and I never saw it again. The Ford Modeling Agency had enough of the drama and told me I needed to find another agency. I had no clothes, no money, and no pictures. A year had passed and things had changed, not only within me and my life, but within the modeling industry as a whole. I found myself at auditions with girls in their teens. I was slightly past the age of thirty and might as well have been a dinosaur. So there I was in New York City, alone. I took my share of meaningless jobs and floundered around in business until I discovered something with the help of my friend, Michael. He was in real estate, converting multi-story brownstones into condominiums. At that time, a lot of partnerships were being created between developers and financial backers. It was a busy time in New York for this type of business. Michael offered me a small job with a smaller salary, and I was thrilled. The office was just around the corner from my apartment. I had recovered enough from my relationship with my ex-husband to start dating again.

Life was looking better. I had started a long-distance relationship with a man named Robert, whom I had dated a few times before I was married. He was a nice man, and I was hopeful that we might have a future together.

Six months into that relationship, I discovered I was pregnant. Me, the one with the tubular issues! I was so excited, I could hardly contain my happiness that I was to have this child. I knew in my heart this was a miracle. I remember walking into the brownstone-conversion office after suffering from a bout of morning sickness. I opened the door to the office and was surprised when I turned on the lights to see one of our clients, a Hassidic man named Ben, sitting in the waiting area. Ben had a habit of arriving thirty minutes before his appointment.

I sat at my small desk across from him as he waited on the bench. He wanted to talk, and I wanted to call Robert and share my news. The minute hand on the clock crawled by as Ben spoke in his soft direct monotone. I prayed that my boss would come to work early so he could take Ben off my hands. He arrived after what seemed a lifetime, and I practically pushed the two men out of the office so I could make my important call.

My heart pounded as the phone rang. After rive rings, Robert picked up. "Hi," I said, barely able to contain my news. "What are you up to?" he said, sounding groggy. He was at home in Colorado and the two-hour time difference meant it was a little after seven in the morning there. I took a deep breath. "I think I'm pregnant." Silence. It was so quiet I could hear my own heart beat.

"Are you sure? Are you sure?" He shot the questions out rapidly, like a machine gun. My head started to spin and I fumbled with the words. "Um. Yes, I think so. I'm going to the doctor today," I stumbled. "I'll pay for the abortion," he stated flatly. My heart collapsed. The fact that I was pregnant was an absolute miracle. I had been told for so many years by doctors that my chances of having a baby were very low. So for me to find out I was carrying a baby after all the physical problems was the most exciting news to me. Instantly I knew I might not have another opportunity to be a mother if I agreed to terminate my pregnancy. I wanted this baby so much. "What? No, I don't think so," I responded. "I want to keep this baby." "Go see the doctor and call me back," he ordered. I didn't say anything else, just softly hung up the phone. I did go to the doctor that afternoon and I was pregnant. I called Robert back later and he insisted I come to Colorado so we could talk things out and "go through this together."

When I got to Colorado I was so relieved to see him, and it felt like we were going to work things out. The first thing we did was go to see his family's doctor. At some point I had the feeling that they were not checking out the pregnancy, but checking to see if I was indeed pregnant. This was not a good sign. When I left Colorado to go see my mother in California, Robert told me we would talk about it. While I was staying at my mother's home, he called me. "If you want to have this baby, I can't stop you," he said, his voice hard and cold. "But I want you to know if that's your decision, then I want nothing to do with you and the baby."

"Are you sure?" I asked. "Maybe you need some time—"

Before I could finish, he cut me off. "Val, I don't want kids. I'm too young anyway, and I'm not ready to be a father. You're on your own if you do this." I hung up the phone. He never spoke to me again. In that moment I wasn't scared. A feeling of peace washed over me. I was actually relieved. I was going to have this child. I was going to raise him or her on my own and on my terms. The freedom was almost giddy. For what felt like the first time in my life I was completely naked to the truth of who I was and what I had to become. I had a miracle growing inside of me that meant more to me than anything.

Once I settled down emotionally, the fear set in. I wasn't doing that great a job of supporting myself, so how was I going to do it for two? You can't do this, the monkey on my shoulder screamed, in the way only he can. "You are not going to be a good mother. You're going to screw this up." Deep down, I knew none of this was true, but it was easy at that moment to let the Monkey run wild in my brain.

I knew I had to get a handle on my thoughts. I knew I had to choose to think positively, but I didn't know how. I struggled with the Monkey. At times, I still do.

While I stayed with my mother in California, my feelings ran the gamut from fear to elation back to fear again. My mother was not in a position to help me financially, and she was no June Cleaver. I was on my own and I knew it. I flew back to New York. My mother had filled my head with warnings. "It's going to be hard," she said. My mother knew how hard it could be, as she had raised four of us on and off on her own.

First, I needed to find a better job. I would need extra money to make it through the first few months after the birth, to pay for my living expenses. I knew that I would need much more money to raise my child, but I tried not to let that completely freak me out. I was offered a job at a large cosmetics company. It was scheduled to begin just after the baby was born, and it would have regular hours so I could manage raising my baby with the salary. There was just one thing; it was in California. I'd like to say I didn't have a choice, but I believe you always have a choice. Even though I didn't want to move to California, I had to choose the right thing for myself and my child.

While I was still in New York, waiting for the baby to be

born, I often walked over to this little church on Sixty-second and Park. It always comforted me to be there. I used to love to sit in the far corner, where I could see the stained glass windows. I would sit and listen, close my eyes and feel my child move inside me. I felt we were a twosome already. I made a promise before God that I would protect this child and do everything in my power to provide him or her with the best life I could.

I would leave the church, and the Monkey would start chattering in my head again. "What are you going to do?" he'd screech. "You're running back to California because you couldn't make it here!" "OH SHUT UP!!!" I blurted out loud. The critical voice in my head spoke to me often. For years I heard it, until I realized the only one who could quiet that voice in my head was me.

It was a Thursday when I went into labor. I took a shower, put on my makeup, curled my hair, and headed to the hospital. After all, I wanted to look good for the birth of my baby! I didn't know what to expect. (As you can imagine, I didn't look so cute by the end of the birth, believe me.) I called Kathleen, my best friend, and she stood there waiting for me at the hospital when I arrived.

Kathleen is one of those women who worry about everything. She is wonderful to have around because she does all the worrying for both of us. Kathleen is the type of friend I could call up at one o'clock in the morning and she would meet me anywhere. One time I called her in the late evening and she had a man in her bed. I asked her to meet me at a party anyway. Twenty minutes later, Kathleen shows up at the party in a ball gown. I asked her what she did with the guy. "Oh, he's asleep," Kathleen shrugged. I laughed. That's Kathleen.

While all the other women had their husbands at the birthing classes, I had Kathleen. "We're going to be parents," she would say to the other couples. The others in the room probably thought we were lesbians. She would just flash this bright Kathleen smile that I still love today. We didn't care. We laughed about everything.

One time I had the opportunity to go fox hunting in Ireland with a man I was dating. I invited Kathleen. "I swear you are Lucy," Kathleen said. "This sounds like another one of your hare-brained adventures." "That makes you Ethel," I replied. And forever more we have become Lucy and Ethel. We did go fox hunting, complete with the feathered hats, jodhpurs, and shiny boots. The men in our lives have come and gone, but our friendship has endured.

My water broke shortly after I reached the hospital, and I was certain I was going to deliver at any moment. However, after seven hours they sent me and Kathleen home because the baby hadn't dropped. My doctor told me to go have a drink to relieve the pain and wait for nature to take its course.

That would never have happened today, but that was the 1980s. At my doctor's suggestion, Kathleen and I headed to Rosa Mexicano on First Avenue, near my apartment. We ordered margaritas and waited for nature to take its course. I felt pretty good after the margaritas until the real labor pains started. I was doing what we learned in birthing class, huffing and puffing—only it was in a bar.

Through the joyous birth of my daughter and the following days, I was always aware of what I would need to begin to consider a life for us. At the drop of a hat, our small apartment in New York was leased to other people and all of a sudden we were on our way to California. That's how I ended up back in California in that little apartment with the borrowed furniture. I learned a lot from that point in my life, but I still had many things to learn, many mistakes to make. And true to myself, I made them all! When I finally left New York, I knew that I wouldn't return for a long time. The one thing that I did know was that I didn't want to return to New York and have people say, "Oh, look at poor Valerie. She lost everything. She can barely make it." Or, "She married some old goat to save herself."

As I sat on the airplane looking out of the window with my baby, Vanessa, on my lap, I knew I wouldn't return until I could hold my head up high. I wouldn't return until I could be someone I was proud of. There are few times in life when you have the luxury to explore fully what you want. As women, we are constantly helping, fixing, nurturing, mending, minding, tending, or being someone or something. Then life hands us an unexpected event—usually a painful one, emotionally or physically.

That is the moment when time stops and for an instant everything is still. It is then that the awakening of the self begins. At first that feeling is fleeting and unfamiliar, but as you nurture it, you grow more powerful by the day. Two events in my life profoundly awoke me to myself—the ending of my marriage and the birth of my daughter. Both experiences created 180-degree shifts in my life and who I thought I was.

Like a diamond in the rough, thousands of pounds of pressure beat away at me until my new self could emerge—shiny, beautiful, and strong.

He who looks outside, dreams.
He who looks inside, awakes.

—CARL JUNG

CHAPTER TWO

Quitting Is Not an Option

Two weeks after I arrived in Los Angeles, the cosmetics job for which I relocated fell through. I was shocked. I had spent money as if I had a job, renting an apartment and buying a used Volkswagen Beetle to get around. True, I needed a place to live and a car no matter what, but I would have rented an even tinier place and bought an even cheaper car. I had to think quickly. What was I going to do for money? I had a few pieces of jewelry left over from modeling that I sold for cash. I hid that money in the bottom of my bedroom closet in a brown leather bag. I treated my closet like a bank and the brown leather bag like a checking account, making withdrawal slips for each amount taken out. Perhaps it was foolish to have kept all the money I had in the world wrapped inside a brown leather bag, but there was so much uncertainty in my life. I needed to know I could get my money as quickly as possible, regardless of the time of day. I needed it close for my own peace of mind. Even though I knew a bank account would be in my name, it was still not the same as having money literally within reach. To this day, I still make sure I have cash available to me. Some habits are hard to let go of.

I did not have enough money for rent, food, car insurance, gas, baby food, and diapers for very long. The only saving grace at that time was the health insurance for myself and my daughter. Thank God for the Screen Actor's Guild! Because of all the commercials I had done, I was eligible for their health insurance program. Without it, I don't know what I would have done; it would have been another payment on top of all the others I couldn't afford. It was crucial to replenish the money I had already spent. Otherwise, my savings, which allowed me eight months of living at the bare minimum, would have been short by several months.

Even though I could live off my jewelry money for a little while it was clear I would need to find a job. I had that brief experience in real estate when I worked for the brownstone conversion company in New York, but realistically, all it qualified me to do was answer phones—not exactly something that would pay enough to support myself and my daughter. The paycheck for answering phones at the brownstone conversion company in New York would only just have covered the cost of diapers and formula.

Part of me wondered if I should go back to New York. The Monkey was at it again, tempting me to find an easier path, though I knew there wasn't anything easier I could do that wouldn't turn out difficult or complicated in the end. With no job skills and no degree, I hardly had a résumé I could wave around town. At least in New York I knew people. I tried to push through my fears, telling myself that I would be okay staying in Los Angeles. I knew I felt better when I was in action than when I was frozen, which gave me time to feel sorry for myself. I had to stop looking back. New York was the past, and in truth, it had been as challenging there as it was in Los Angeles, just in a different way. I knew I had two strengths: my personality and my perseverance. My good friend Jonathan recognized this too. It was Jonathan who suggested that I go into real estate. He had been very successful at it and believed that I had the potential to be successful as well.

We had been in Los Angeles six months. Just as everything was crumbling around me, Jonathan was visiting me from New York. All I could offer him was a folding chair as he sat in my tiny apartment. I would have been embarrassed if I had not been so completely filled with anxiety. I was sitting on the borrowed sofa, and Vanessa began to cry. The evening sun was setting in the distance, but you would never know it because there was nothing but a murky stream of light flowing into the room. I began explaining why I was living in this place. I tried to tell him that I was unemployed and struggling just to pay the rent. I wanted to hold my head up. I wanted to finish my story, but instead I started to cry. He listened intently, looking around for a tissue to offer me, but there wasn't one. Nor was there a table to hold the tissue box. Instead, I used my hand to rub the tears from my cheeks while struggling to regain my composure.

"I have a great idea!" he exclaimed, his voice echoing in the empty room.

By this time I had picked up Vanessa and was trying to soothe her with a bottle. My daughter fussed and kicked for a few moments and finally began to settle down as I rocked her.

"What, win the lottery?" I asked, taking a deep breath. "Slip and fall in the supermarket maybe?" My jokes fell flat. I wasn't feeling cheery, but I needed to lighten the mood. I didn't want my friend to see how truly devastated I was, though my tears were hardly convincing him otherwise.

"You are going to go into real estate," he said. "Residential real estate. You'll sell houses; you'll be great at it!"

"Houses? I don't know anything about selling houses. I was a model, remember?" I cried.

"Take it a step at a time," he said. "You'll start by getting your real estate license and go from there."

He made it sound so easy. I didn't have any other ideas of what I could do. I didn't have anything pulling me one way or the other. I took a deep breath and dried my tears. I thought about everything that Jonathan had been telling me. He was one of the calmest people I had ever met, and he made a lot of sense. I made the decision at that moment to Just Do It, as the Nike ad says. You know, all it takes is one person to believe in you so much and then you can move forward and believe in yourself. You could call it blind faith that propelled me forward to a real estate career, but maybe it was the hug I got from Jonathan when I was all cried out that told me I could go on. Does it really matter? If I'd paused even for a moment to question my ability or the idea too much, I might never have taken the step I did toward changing the direction of my life.

Seven days later, I was going to classes at night to get my real estate license. During the day I worked as a real estate assistant, trying to learn as much as I could. For the first time in my life, I made a solid commitment to myself. It was during those times that I began to understand the challenges a single working mother confronts daily. I couldn't afford day care for Vanessa. So I traded hours of child care with my neighbors. I would watch their kids on the weekends, and they would watch Vanessa for some portion of the day during the week. In the morning I'd pack her bag: diapers, six bottles, formula, two blankets, a pacifier, change of clothes, toys, and her favorite stuffed animal, a fluffy pink elephant that squeaked. Then I'd feed her from her bassinet on the bathroom counter while I did my makeup. Once in the car, I'd hurriedly comb through my hair while looking in the rearview mirror. On the weekends I had double or triple the gear, juggling the diaper bag, my work bag, and other people's kids to make it through my day.

On most days, I'd leave the office at 2:30 p.m., pick Vanessa up from my neighbor, and bring her back to work with me. I sat at a large mahogany desk, home to an empty Rolodex, a telephone, and a blank sheet of paper. It was also a sanctuary for Vanessa and me. She slept or played with her toys underneath my desk, on her blanket, while I worked. I loved having her there. And fortunately, she was a very easy baby. From 3:00 p.m. until we left the office at 7:00 p.m., this was her second home. Since I was not licensed and could not show or sell houses, I sat there all day doing whatever I could to justify my meager paycheck. The money helped cover a few of my expenses. To make myself feel better I took one of the office's business cards and wrote my name on it. Underneath my name I wrote "Assistant to the President." It worked, temporarily, to give me some credibility. I became a master at juggling schedules and multitasking. At one point I found myself talking on the phone, filling out a contract, and pushing a little swing with Vanessa in it with my foot while eating lunch. If it meant landing a deal and getting a bonus check, I would have found a way to skip rope too! Determination was the name of the game.

At least I got my license. However, I was scared all the time. No matter how many hours I put in, I wasn't closing any deals. I wasn't selling any homes. Money was going out faster than it was coming in. I needed two new tires a few months after I arrived in Los Angeles. Buying those two new tires cost me *one month's earnings*. And then my car engine began to overheat. Every unscheduled expense tossed me into a hurricane of anxiety. My mind would not stop racing with worry.

There was not one single hour in the day that I wasn't trying to figure out how I was going to take care of Vanessa and sell real estate. It's all that ran through my mind. "Keep going, Valerie, keep going, Valerie" became my mantra.

Nights were the worst. Vanessa would be sleeping soundly like an angel, blissfully unaware of the enormous pressures that regularly engulfed me. I would vacuum the same stretch of carpet over and over like a maniac. The monotonous hum of the machine kept my fear at bay. I folded the same laundry over and over. I washed and rewashed dishes at two o'clock in the morning. I would clean until I literally fell into bed, exhausted.

Fear and anxiety had become my unwanted companions. In the mornings, when I would have to leave Vanessa with my neighbor, seeing her little outstretched hand and hearing her loud cries would break my heart. I'd turn to leave, wishing there could have been another way for us, but there wasn't one that didn't cost an even higher price than the two of us being briefly separated. I had to work for us to survive.

Those mornings were terrible. It was like someone was ripping out my heart. I would see Vanessa's tear-streaked face as I left her, and that vision haunted my day. Many times it was really hard to handle the everyday ups and downs. But I did. My commitment to escaping the traps of the past, when I had been dependent on someone else, and my desire to be a great mother and provider for Vanessa gave me strength when I felt like I did not have any at all.

Clients would call up and yell at me for not knowing the answers to their questions. The mechanic would call me repeatedly, trying to get paid for the repairs on my car he had made as I rationed out the little money I had left. I'm not telling you this to make you feel sorry for me. I'm telling you this because it was my life. Life can seem unfair and many times complicated. Looking back, I realize those were the experiences that I needed to appreciate the beautiful moments I did have in my life. One night, I lay awake in bed, too exhausted to clean, too exhausted to sleep. It had been one of those days. I got up and walked across the room to Vanessa. She was so perfect. I stroked her soft pink cheek. I stood there motionless and watched her breathe, her tiny chest rising steadily in her pink flannel nightgown. I loved smelling her. Whenever I smelled her soft baby scent a feeling of peace would wash over me. She was my everything. I hoped that one day my daughter would be proud of me. I wanted her to look back at our life together and know that I made a good life for us without selling my soul. "I love you, my little angel," I whispered to her as I returned to bed.

Nine months passed without a single home sale. I was being swallowed up by debt. I didn't know what to do. I didn't know where to turn. I became increasingly anxious. I prayed that something would come to me—some new thought, some new vision, some direction. Finally it did come, when I least expected it. The phone rang one afternoon, and it was Jonathan, the friend who had recommended I go into real estate. He wanted to know how I was doing. "Something is wrong with me," I explained as I began to cry. "I haven't sold a thing! I can't do this. I'm not getting anywhere." "Okay. Okay," he soothed. "I'm calling because I'm coming into town tomorrow. Let's have dinner; we'll figure it out." I put the phone back on the cradle before sliding down the wall onto the floor. I had to have faith, blind faith, to keep going. I knew I couldn't quit, though I didn't know what else to do. I anxiously awaited the help Jonathan was offering. I was thankful I had told him the truth and asked for his help. I could have asked for his help earlier, but I had been so immersed in the chaos, it hadn't occurred to me that reaching out was an option. After all that I had been facing, my old sense of pride had melted away, and I felt no shame asking for help anymore. It was the only way I was going to learn.

The next night we met for dinner. Jonathan asked me to walk him through my day.

"Well, these people call and ask me all these questions about houses and they are so rude. They're nasty, actually. Jonathan, I'm doing the best that I can. I have my baby sleeping under my desk while I'm trying to work, and learn, and pay my bills. Can't they tell how hard I'm trying? They can't talk to me like that!"

"So what do you do?" he asked.

"I give it back to them," I said hotly. "They can't talk to me like that." He looked stunned. I kept talking.

"Sometimes, I yell at them and tell them to listen and to stop screaming at me."

"Then what?" he asked, barely disguising his horrified look. I was speaking so fast, so emotionally, that I didn't realize he was looking at me like I had done something wrong. "What do you do?"

"I hang up on them! I slam the phone down in their ear." I grinned. "I showed *them*."

"Val, you're not going to make any money that way," he said, shaking his head. "Most people buying or selling homes are really stressed. This is the largest purchase or sale they will ever make in their lives. This can make them very emotional. They are looking to *you* for support, for guidance. They need *you* to lead them through the difficult sales process." He explained patiently as if to a small child. "You can't yell at them and you can't hang up on them."

"But they hurt my feelings," I said. "I'm doing my best."

I was doing the very best that I could, and nobody seemed to recognize this. The clients were angry; I was angry. With less than a year in real estate, it felt like I couldn't do any more than I was doing. He took my hand. "You can't take these things personally. This is not about you. This is about them, all about them. They are the clients." I finally began to understand my first hard lesson in business. I realized I needed to soothe the clients. I needed to understand more about what they needed. Jonathan was making sense.

Looking back, I can only laugh at myself. How did I not know that? It's amazing when you start opening your mind and seeking answers. Just the mere act of asking for help or the seeking out of a better way to live can be enough to create a small shift in your life. That's how it started for me. It was such a release when I finally let go, recognizing that I couldn't do it all. When I finally realized that admitting I needed help didn't make me weak, it made me stronger, help began to come from unexpected places. It was my prayers that brought me Jonathan. I was grateful for his guidance.

I was beginning to feel like I had taken a big step toward a real estate career. I wish I had had the same guidance about how to be a single parent. At the time I wanted to be a perfect mother, whatever that was supposed to mean. Anytime I failed my idea of perfection I was torn with guilt and self-doubt. It was Fourth of July weekend when an opportunity arose for me to be the agent representing an entire building. The client had planned an impromptu meeting with five of his lawyers and was expecting a representative from our company to be there. The agent that had brought the deal in had had a car accident and was in the hospital.

Everyone else was busy for the holiday weekend, except me. I had dreamed about making a large sale, but I didn't imagine it would happen so quickly. This was my opportunity! But you can guess what it was like trying to find a sitter for Vanessa on that popular weekend. I called everyone I could think of who I trusted to sit with Vanessa for a few hours. No one answered their home phone. Those who did were busy. I was consumed by the thought that if I managed to make this deal happen, I could finally get on my feet. *I can handle this*, I told myself. I knew what I had to do. I would have to take Vanessa with me. It was about ninety degrees in L.A. that day. Vanessa was toddling around in a little sundress. I, however, having made no money, had to wear my clothes from New York. I didn't have a light summer suit, I had a heavy one. Imagine me, boiling in the oppressive Los Angeles heat in my wool jacket, wool pants, and a light wool sweater. And to complete my heat stroke ensemble, I wore the only matching shoes—boots, ankle length—that I had. They were suede. The rest of my good clothes had been kept or destroyed by my ex, and though I had a few summer sundresses, I had nothing that made me look professional. I strapped Vanessa in her car seat, and with the air-conditioning blasting, we were on our way.

When I arrived, the client and his lawyers were seated outside around a large lawn table a few yards away from the pool. I looked around quickly, trying to find some shade. My suit was dark and collecting heat like a convection oven. I tried to think cool, but the sweat began to run down my back as my clothes stuck to my skin. I smiled my best smile, trying not to show how feverishly hot I was. I put Vanessa on the grass. Soon she was barefoot and running around playing with her toys, entertaining herself with a butterfly that flitted by. The client's family and friends and a few other children lounged around the pool, enjoying the heat.

As the meeting began, Vanessa was sitting on the patio next to me, playing with her dolls and coloring. In a flash, she jumped up and tried to grab the butterfly she had seen before. In doing so, she fell in the pool, with me immediately diving in after her.

I had no thought, at least none I can remember. I saw nothing but my child under the water. I heard nothing except the monkey on my shoulder screaming, "Vanessa! She's going to drown!" My heart was racing when I pulled her above the waterline. She was sputtering and coughing. I could tell she was looking to me for a way to react. I held her up and said,

"Wheeee! Isn't this fun! What a good diver! Oh my goodness, look at you. You're all wet!" I was standing in the pool with my boots on and my jacket floating on top of the water. My heart was racing and my hands were shaking as I held her up. The water from my hair ran down my face, melting my makeup.

It helped mask the tears that threatened to overflow from my relief that she was okay. I knew if I let her sense how upset I was, it would only increase her stress or make her afraid of the water. Instead I tried to make it a fun moment. All the lawyers and our client were standing around the pool, looking horrified. Everything happened so fast. I climbed out of the pool and, of course, I didn't have any dry clothes with me. But I had to finish the meeting. My face was a wreck, my mascara smeared under my eyes, my hair hanging in my face, dripping and smelling of chlorine. The chlorine at least cut the scent of drenched wool, which made me smell like a wet dog. The client's son, who was a big guy, had a big white T-shirt and an extra pair of boxer shorts. I changed out of my soggy clothes and finished the meeting in boxer shorts and a big white T-shirt, Vanessa gurgling on my lap.

Once we had returned home, I lay with her in my arms until she fell asleep. When she was sleeping soundly, I cried my eyes out while I washed the chlorine from my hair. "What are you doing?" the monkey on my shoulder screeched. "Vanessa could have died today and it's all your fault! You made a mess today, Valerie! A real mess!" I sat down on the floor of the cramped shower, letting the water rain down on me. "Go back to New York. You can't do this on your own," the Monkey continued, louder than he had ever been before. I argued with the Monkey, even though I continued to cry my eyes out. "No, I can do this! I saved her when she fell in. Quitting is not an option."

That was the single worst incident that happened when she was a toddler. I would never forget it. It was easy taking her with me, and I loved having her with me, but from that moment on, I became more protective, more watchful. Being a single mom is hard. No feeling in the world can compare with the profound love you feel for your child, but it doesn't change the fact that it sometimes requires you to push yourself to total mental and physical exhaustion.

When you are a single parent, the final decision is up to you. There is no spouse to bounce ideas off of, no one else to share the responsibility for mistakes. Parenting is really about your choices. Ultimately, children are a reflection of the person who raised them. One of the hardest things about being a single parent is that there is often no relief. No one to hand your baby to when you have had enough, or when you are sick, or when you are sad, or if you just need a little space. You have to find the strength to be both mother and father to your child. Somehow you manage to do it. We are amazing that way. Single parents do it all. We diaper, we feed, we budget, we pay, we work, we clean; we do everything.

I didn't get the deal that day, in case you are wondering. I don't know if it was my swim in their pool, the boxer shorts, or the fact that I showed up with a baby. I just know

I didn't get it. Since the building deal didn't work out, I turned my attention back to trying to list homes. I collected phone numbers of all the developers by driving around in the afternoons, copying down the numbers off their signs, and then calling them once I was back in the office. I called developer after developer, day after day, pleading for a meeting. This went on for several months. Finally, one agreed. It was my sheer persistence that got me the meeting. I had called repeatedly, pestering his office for an appointment. I was enthusiastic, telling them how many times I had been to the house, describing and offering suggestions about the interior. I had to prove my value so they would meet with me. "Why should we meet with you? You're new, and we already have relationships with other brokers," they'd reply. "I can bring you a new perspective. I will put all the energy I have into this project," I'd respond. I never mentioned that I would be accompanied by my baby. I was finally on my way to meet my first developer and with luck to list my first house.

I arrived at the developer's office with no time to spare. Vanessa had thrown herself out of her crib the night before, and I had awoken to a loud thud and screams. I didn't want to leave her in her crib again, so I had brought her into my bed to sleep with me. An hour later, she finally fell asleep. Two hours later I had overslept, and I had scrambled that morning to get myself together to make this very important appointment. I was walking up the stairs to the office, carrying Vanessa on one hip, her diaper bag with the usual supplies, plus her crayons and coloring books, on my shoulder, while negotiating my briefcase in my free hand as I attempted to hold on to the handrail with my pinky finger. Just as I opened the door to walk in, my heel broke. It didn't just crack, hanging slightly from the rest of the shoe. It snapped completely off! Three inches of my shoe lay abandoned on the step. I balanced precariously on one foot, trying to control Vanessa, who was wiggling around trying to look at everything. I couldn't possibly bend over and pick it up without the receptionist seeing the whole thing. I also didn't want to fall over with my bags, my baby, and my broken shoe.

So there I was, teetering on one high heel and balancing on one flat shoe. I stood at the reception desk on my tiptoes and asked to see the developer. Suddenly, the developer's secretary appeared and said, "He's ready to see you now." I didn't have a moment to pick up the broken heel that I had kicked just inside the door, so I had to leave it behind. I was thinking more about the heel than the fact that I was standing there holding my daughter and all my stuff. It had its bright side, though, because it didn't give me any time to be nervous. The secretary didn't notice my shoe, but was instead looking at me holding my baby and bags. I guess, looking back, I was quite a sight.

She motioned me down the hall. As she turned her back, I kicked off both my shoes and quickly bent over to pick them up. I stuffed them out of sight into my open diaper bag. I walked into the office in my stocking feet. When I was introduced, I looked the developer square in the eye, to keep his attention away from my feet. The desk between us helped. I quickly sat down. I muttered something about having a sick babysitter, which was my ongoing story, and I put Vanessa on the floor next to me with her crayons and paper. I hid my feet under my chair and started talking. After the meeting was over, I was picking up all the things off the floor, including Vanessa, when he came from around his desk and saw that I had no shoes on. He looked at my stocking feet but said nothing. "On the way up the stairs, I tripped and broke the heel off of one of my shoes," I nervously explained. "I don't let anything stop me." I rambled on for a few more minutes, trying to tell him how hard I would work on his project and that nothing, not even a broken shoe, would get in my way. He just smiled at me as I chattered away. He was a kind man with kind eyes. In the end he gave me a chance by letting me hold Sunday open houses at the house once it was finished. With my bare feet and my baby in tow, someone was giving me a chance.

Even though my career was looking up, my personal life was beginning to come unraveled. I couldn't keep up with my housework. My place was a mess. The manic vacuuming had stopped; dishes were piling up. I was spending so much time on my business that my home life suffered. All I could do was keep Vanessa neat and clean and get myself out the door. I noticed a rancid smell coming from my bedroom closet one night. I was nearing complete exhaustion and was sure the smell was that of decaying rats in the wall.

As I frantically tried to balance home, work, and caring

for my baby, I began to see myself shushing Vanessa. For the first time, I lost my patience and attempted to quiet my daughter while I was on the phone with a potential client. "Vanessa, please! Mommy is on the phone," I hissed as I covered the receiver with my hand. I knew my tone of voice was wrong; it just came out of my mouth that way before I could stop it.

A previous argument with my apartment manager only added to the pressure. I had called him upset by the health hazard dead rats could present to Vanessa. "There are dead rats in the wall behind the closets! I can smell their dead bodies! I have a baby!" I yelled over the telephone.

"I'm sorry, Miss Fitzgerald; the exterminators can't come until Monday afternoon."

"Monday afternoon? I have to be at work. Why can't they come now?" "They can come sooner, but that will be an extra five hundred dollars, which you'd have to pay." "What! I have a toddler living in a rat-infested apartment and you're telling me that I have to wait out the weekend with this stench and I have to pay? What kind of man are you?"

"Look, Miss Fitzgerald, I'll see what I can do about getting them there sooner, but you're still going to have to pay the fee. And it'll be more if I can get them there tonight."

"I can't afford to pay them." "You can add it to next month's rent, Miss Fitzgerald. That's the best I can do."

"Fine, call them." I hung up. I had no way to pay them, though it was some relief knowing I at least had a month to figure it out. The exterminators arrived later that night and tore out the back wall of my closet. They found where the stench was coming from. It wasn't rats in the wall; it was sour milk from the baby bottles I had forgotten and left in my jacket pockets. I was so embarrassed for the way I had acted. I was equally furious with myself for wasting so much money.

It was then that I realized I needed more help than Jonathan could offer. All the chaos and pressures in my life were getting to me. I wasn't sleeping properly, I was having anxiety attacks, I was fearful, in debt, and my emotions were getting the best of me. Something in my life needed to change, and it needed to change quickly. I had a choice to make. I could either choose to marry and let someone take care of me for the rest of my life, with all the strings attached, or I could commit myself to learn as much as I could about running a business so that I could create the life I wanted for me and my daughter. I needed to get organized, quiet the chaos and the drama going on in my head, and focus!

Now that you know my story I think that you can see that if a little girl from South Dakota could create an abundant life, you can too. The remainder of this book is dedicated to sharing with you the thoughts, the tips, and the techniques of all the powerful people who influenced my career. I want to share with you how, by surrendering to the concept that I didn't need to know everything, I achieved success. Great people learn from and surround themselves with smart people. Perhaps that is one of the reasons my business was recently ranked thirty-fourth nationwide in the *Wall Street Journal* for sales success.

No matter what the circumstances are in your life, you can make decisions that can help you create the life you want!

All we are is a result of what we have thought.

—THE BUDDHA

CHAPTER THREE

What I Needed to Know

How did I begin my real estate career and go from struggling to making ends meet to making millions? It took a leap of faith and a lot of determination and the belief that I could and would succeed. As a single mother, for the sake of my child and my own well-being, I pushed the Monkey aside and managed my inner stress. I consciously made choices to change our lives and improve our circumstances.

I let go of the tremendous demands that I put upon myself to be the perfect blend of homemaker, breadwinner, mother, father, teacher, coach and just got out there and took action. I stopped getting ready to get ready. I flew out of the starting block. Building a business takes courage, and I knew that I had to be resourceful and strong. I had to consider the well-being of Vanessa and the future that I hoped to provide for both of us.

A real estate career offered me the opportunity to make my dreams come true. I mapped out a juggling act fit for the circus. I set up a schedule with my neighbor to watch each other's children. That gave me a measure of flexibility to work extra hours at the office on certain days. Other days, I took the kids with me. I set down the rules of the day and off we went to work. Our first stop was always the drive-through for breakfast at McDonald's. I guess you could say the children were my first assistants. I enjoyed taking the kids with me everywhere, to the office and to showings. One of my first leadership experiences was leading four three-year-olds on a showing of a vacant multimillion-dollar house. They were screaming with glee to be in a huge open space with no furniture. While most of the children were exploring the rooms, my daughter came running up to me just as the buyers walked into the front door. "Mommy, Mommy, the house smells like someone died here." I laughed and said, "Isn't she cute," and then I said to Vanessa, "Go find your friends." You'd be surprised how many of the people I met along the way when I had the kids with me were actually supportive and complimentary of my effort.

Proper preparation and organization were key elements to my success. As Vanessa grew inch by inch, my business grew client by client. You must prepare yourself to handle life as you grow and change. Remaining calm under pressure and stress positively affects your decision-making abilities and keeps you focused on your end goal. Map out your day. Anticipate the unexpected, and leave room for possible last-minute change of plans. Don't become emotionally attached.

Seek help if a solution doesn't present itself. Take every opportunity to learn from those whom you most respect. When you decide you want a career in real estate, you need to understand the necessary steps to create the successful business and the life that you envision. So let's begin building your business by preparing you to tackle stressful situations in positive ways.

Stress Management

Mounting strains from deadlines, self-imposed expectations, perceived external pressures, and responsibilities can pile up before you realize it. However, it is entirely possible to defuse a stressful situation before it gets to the boiling point. It's a simple matter of being aware, alert, and prepared. Your ability to function productively depends in a large part on your stress-management skills. When I needlessly yelled at my apartment manager, insisting there were rats in my walls, when employing a normal tone of voice would have been sufficient to resolve the problem, I was clearly under a high level of stress. When I hung up on potential clients and other real estate agents, I acted out of a lack of understanding about how to manage stress. I had to learn to develop systems that worked for me to alleviate the pressure and allow me to act in more responsible ways to achieve my goals.

Just the other day, I had a client call me about his house. He was very upset because it hadn't sold and he was screaming at me. I had known this client for many years and had

represented him in the sale and purchase of multiple properties. I knew that he had faith and trust in me or he wouldn't
have remained loyal throughout the years. I also knew that
he had a temper. I learned long ago never to fight fire with
fire. I waited for the client to wear himself out; he was then
able to calm down. Having given him no feedback about
what I was thinking or feeling, he had no way to affect me
negatively. I hadn't used any of my energy and had captured
all of his. I was so calm and collected that it put me at an advantage. The phone call finished on a high note and a good
laugh and an apology from the client.

I recall one time a buyer was so nervous about buying
her first home, it seemed like every time we spoke her voice
would start off in a normal tone and within seconds she
would be screaming. Since I had several of these conversations each day with her, they were beginning to be very
stressful for me. One day I just couldn't bear the screaming
from her, so I interrupted the discussion and told her that I
needed to put her on hold. I knew that if I didn't create some
distance, I would blow my top. My intention was to put her
on hold to give myself a few seconds to calm down, maybe
even count to ten. I put down the phone, and sitting at my
desk, let out a scream of curse words that would rival any
heard in a barroom brawl. For a moment I felt better, until I
heard her voice coming out of the phone. In complete shock
and horror I realized that I had forgotten to press the hold
button. Of course she demanded to know if I had been
screaming at her. I replied, "Of course not!" I told her that
something awful had happened while I was talking to her

and I had been reacting to that. Of course I could never let her know what really happened. The lesson in all of this is not to hang on to stress, let it out—and don't forget to press the hold button!

There are many stressful situations, and the best way to manage stress is to evaluate what works best for you and those with whom you do business. Know your limits and the limitations of your clients. Be aware, be alert, and be present. Don't let it get out of hand and turn into a five-alarm fire.

An important way to get a handle on your stress is to establish a routine schedule. Being organized will give you a sense of being able to maneuver during random and high-pressure situations. In the evening, make a list of everything you need to get done the next day. Write in pencil so that when deadlines and urgent matters arise you can erase and move things around in order of their priority. Whenever you're feeling stressed, stop, take a deep breath, and count to ten. Implement ways to relieve stress that fit your personality.

Once you've mapped out your day, you can rearrange appointments when unexpected situations need your immediate attention. Take a deep breath, reflect, and think the situation through. Take action in a calm and orderly way. Don't lose your composure. Be mindful to insure that your actions make a positive contribution to the situation. Implementation of these steps will lower your stress level, raise your level of productivity, and increase your potential for success.

REFLECTIONS: WAYS OF COPING WITH STRESS

▶ Let off steam in a positive way.

▶ Count to ten.

▶ Don't engage in a heated conversation.

▶ Know your limits.

▶ Exercise.

▶ Take some time to relax.

▶ Get enough sleep.

▶ Be prepared and organized.

▶ Don't be afraid to ask for help.

How You Think

When you change your mindset, you change your life. A lot of people think that life is just a series of random events and coincidences. I believe that there are no coincidences in life and that everything matters and has a purpose. Every thought, every spoken word, and every action is important. You are the person you see in the mirror. You are the voice you hear in your head. You have the power to think positively, to encourage yourself and act responsibly and swiftly. No one can take that from you.

Having a positive state of mind is the difference between having just enough and having a life of abundance.

▶ **PASSION.**

Passionate people are dedicated people. They are tenacious and relentlessly pursue their goal.

▶ **COMMITMENT.**

Committed people are reliable people. They are accountable until the end, through all the ups and downs, no matter what.

▶ **DETERMINATION.**

Determined people are strong people. They don't waver. They walk the walk.

It is normal to have some doubts; we all have them in varying degrees at one time or another. As I've mentioned, I call these thoughts the "monkey on my shoulder." The monkey on my shoulder would tell me, "You can't, you're not good enough. It will never work." This critical voice zeros in on all the insecurities we have as mothers and businesswomen. Eventually, I realized that I could control that voice and subsequently my thoughts changed from *How am I going to provide for Vanessa, I don't know what I'm doing* to *I will make a great life for my daughter, I know everything will work out.* That empowerment changed both my real estate career and my life. It focused my thoughts and energy on what was good in my life and what could make my life better. Realizing that I could turn my world around made a huge difference. I stopped hitting my head against the wall and simply moved a few inches to the side to find the opening to propel my career forward.

I had a whole new outlook on life. It was bright and sunny. The house with the eight-foot ceilings was now vaulted with skylights. When clients demanded answers and lost their tempers, instead of viewing them as mean, impatient people who had no idea how hard I was trying, I understood that all they really wanted from me was to solve their problem. I became that problem solver.

You become what you believe. This concept is repeated over and over throughout history. Every repetitive thought you have is an affirmation. Choose to affirm positive ones. Focus on the vision or the thought that empowers you. If you want to have a beautiful house someday, then visualize yourself in the beautiful house. How many bedrooms does it have? What style is it? What does it feel like when you put the keys in the front door for the first time? You can have what you want. Visualization is a way of preparing for the reality you want to create.

When you utilize visualization you become energized. It's important to keep that energy focused. Buy a magazine, look at pictures. Tear out a photo that speaks to you and put it on your wall. Create a vision board.

Once you feel it and see it, it becomes your reality. The energy flows and you feel yourself closing in on your goal. I always say that there is no end game, just a series of goals. Remember, Rome wasn't built in one day, and you can't accomplish all your goals at once. Your compounded victories will give you a stronger, deeper foundation, enabling you to build higher and higher. Stay positive. Every time you start feeling down or distracted, pull up the vision of what you want. Remind yourself of your goal. Go out, buy another magazine, imagine what it would be like if you were ready to buy your dream home now. Every idea, invention, or dream begins with a desire for something better, the courage to face a challenge, and the passion to get it done.

REFLECTIONS: STAYING YOUR COURSE

▶ Make your work your passion.

▶ Develop the desire to succeed.

▶ Be an independent thinker.

▶ Have a positive attitude.

▶ Develop self-discipline.

▶ Have integrity.

▶ Cultivate good people skills.

Beginning the Journey

People enter real estate sales from many different circumstances. They may have tried many jobs or careers before deciding to get a real estate license. As you know, I was in a critical place in my life with no business experience or contract experience, living in a new environment where I was just getting to know people.

If you are interested in real estate, find a local real estate training school where you can take classes. They may even offer a choice of day or evening classes where you can learn the basics that will get you ready to take your state's real estate exam. Start investigating real estate offices in your spare time. Ultimately, you will need to place your license with a real estate company. In many circumstances, most states will hold your license until you have found a broker or company.

Selecting the Right Company

Choose a company and setting that is right for you. Envision yourself in the office. Make it a solid fit to reflect your goals and aspirations. Ask yourself important questions and interview yourself before you interview with offices. These are some questions you may want to ask yourself or ask when you interview with an office. Ask about their training programs. What are the fees associated with working there? What kind of help do they offer agents in finding business? Who in their management team will help you with any questions or concerns with buyers and sellers? What kind of work space and equipment do they offer? Are the offices somewhere you would be proud to bring your buyers and sellers? What's the commission split?

Carefully think about your options and prioritize your needs. In the beginning, because you are a newly licensed agent, you'll need to rely on your company's reputation to help establish your own. When visiting the offices for your interview, observe the agents. Are they working together, are they friendly toward one another? Is there more of a competitive edge to the office environment? Which scenario would work best for your personality? Are you a team player or more of a lone ranger? How are the agents dressed? Are they dressed casually, or are more agents dressed in business attire? Ask the manager or person interviewing you if you could attend an office meeting. It's important to take in the tone of the office to better judge if you'll feel comfortable working there. Look at the work spaces. Are the desks close together or is there a feeling of roominess? Are there private offices for agents? Are the offices separated from the desks on the main floor? Do you respond to light? If so, are there windows in the office? Not every real estate office has windows for everyone. Often the best-positioned desks are given to leading agents as a sign of respect or a reward for production.

When I first started, I didn't see my office as the place I would be spending a lot of time. My office could have been almost anywhere I could do business. It could have been my apartment or my car. There was no window in any of my offices for thirteen years. The only view I had was of my vision board. On that vision board were pictures of the life I was creating. One was a picture of a home and another was a beach house. It was full of images I wanted in my life; it was my window.

Think about it, I was in real estate for thirteen years before I had a real window. However, the view that fed me the most, and still does, is the one that comes from my vision board.

REFLECTIONS: QUESTIONS TO ASK WHEN INTERVIEWING

► What kind of training programs do you offer?

► What are the fees associated with working here?

► What kind of help do you offer agents in finding business?

► How many agents will show up to an open house?

► What's your company's orientation process?

► Who in management will help me with any questions or concerns with buyers and sellers?

► What kind of work space and equipment do you offer?

► What's the commission split?

Seeking Guidance

People do business with those with whom they can relate. They gravitate toward agents they think are strong, hardworking, confident, and smart. Getting along in an office is a talent in and of itself. Creating a network of agents and establishing a positive reputation among them is crucial to your success. Carry yourself with pride, not arrogance. Never be afraid to admit what you don't know. Seek out a mentor; ask an experienced agent for advice. Don't spend time reinventing the wheel. Your day will be filled with much more important things to do.

Recognizing that I needed a mentor was a turning point in my career. With no sales in nine months, I knew that I wasn't doing things as I should, but I didn't know what to do next or how to fix the problem. Every day I was sitting at my desk, trying to fill my empty Rolodex, a sleeping baby at my feet. A top saleswoman and leader in my company stopped to say hello. She was smart, dynamic, and successful. I admired this woman. I sheepishly asked her advice. She was friendly and frank. In a flash of a smile she solved my problem. She gave me the secret of her success: It was having a mentor. She told me that when she started she had a mentor who knew the business and gave her lots of ideas to help her succeed. Wow, all I wanted was to make one sale, bring in one commission check and I would be thrilled! So I listened attentively and knew in my heart she was right.

When I first started modeling, I didn't know how to stand, how to smile, or how to walk a runway, so I watched the more successful models. I closed my Murphy bed and practiced walking around my tiny studio apartment. I flipped through hundreds of magazines, studying the way women carried themselves. I needed to employ that same technique in my real estate business.

Fortunately, my desk was positioned where I could watch and listen as I worked. I took note of the conversations of the more established real estate agents. I observed them with their clients, listened to the words they chose and the way they delivered news to their clients.

In the beginning of my career, a deal I had in the works was falling apart. I had an accepted offer on a house and was certain that it would close successfully. One day, I received a phone call from the agent who represented the buyers. He explained that due to unforeseen problems, the buyers could not procure a loan. Therefore, they would not be in a position to purchase the home. I had to call my clients, the sellers, and tell them the bad news. I thought they would be angry and prepared myself for the worst. I decided to try what I had learned by watching and listening to the other agents. I calmly gave my clients the news in a matter-of-fact manner. I was sympathetic without being dramatic. I made no excuses and delivered the news in a professional tone and expressed a positive belief that the house would sell again.

As it turned out, the sellers were relieved. They had what we call "seller's remorse." They thanked me for my hard work, appreciated my honesty, diligence, and integrity. They stayed in their house but became a wonderful source of referrals. They were so happy with my representation and felt that I had handled the situation with such poise and grace that they told all of their friends to work with me. I had learned a valuable lesson from those more established agents: The news is just the news.

It's important if you are new in the field of real estate to find and follow a mentor. Look for someone who has coached others to success. The person you should seek out is someone believable, credible, and ethical. Be mindful to choose a mentor with a positive attitude who has a love for the real estate business and who will take the time to share her thoughts and ideas with you. Many new agents learn by assisting more experienced agents. Ask your mentor if you can be helpful to her. Ask if you can accompany your mentor to meetings with buyers and sellers and to open houses. It's a great opportunity to learn the real estate business firsthand.

As children, we don't often get to choose our mentors. As adults, we can decide to listen to the voice of reason or the voice of delusion. We can choose to be guided by a positive or negative voice. I have had the good fortune to have been mentored by intelligent, thoughtful agents and have had a wonderfully talented coach for the last eight years. We all need a little advice, sometimes a friendly reminder or two, and once in a while a kick in the pants!

I pulled from the collective intelligence and experience of the agents around me to build my knowledge base. How do you keep a winning mind-set? By focusing on your goals and remembering you are in real estate to accomplish things for all parties. Celebrate your small victories as you go. In the beginning a victory may be as simple as having a successful call with a client, being able to answer their questions or understand what it is they are looking for in a home. Remember: You are a leader, and by buying this book, you are learning what you need to do to lead your life in a new direction.

REFLECTIONS: GUIDANCE TIPS

▶ Observe the top producer in your office to see how she works day in and day out.

▶ Ask an experienced agent if you could spend time with him during the day or shadow him on his appointments.

Power Source

As with anything in life, it is important to reflect carefully on the "why" of your pursuits and actions. In this case you need to consider the "why" of your goal to take on a real estate career. This clarity will help you through the challenging moments. There will be times when you will go from superhero in your client's eyes to villain because she may believe that you aren't representing her interests. There will be people who will expect, and even want, an adversarial experience that may challenge your representation of them. Many clients are unaware of the tremendous amount of responsibility that you carry for them in a transaction.

The "why" is the power source that will get you through these moments. Moreover, it will be the power source that drives you to your ultimate dreams.

I am aware that Vanessa was my power source. This is the reason why in the beginning of my career when someone said no to me, it engaged all my senses. In fact, I would get so excited that there was an objection to my ideas, I would rally all my resources to change the prospect's thinking. As time progressed, the goals I set for myself were achieved. My daughter was having the life I had envisioned for her, and I was on my way to becoming the businesswoman I am today.

One day, my confidence and skills became my power source. It took time to implement my years of learning, as it will for you. You must take the time to learn the business. One of the benefits of focusing on doing your job well is developing the habits that constitute a perfect day for you. Repetition is the quickest way to learn anything. Re-create steps that empower you. For me, the pride and care with which I was able to care for my clients fed not only my power source but my clients' confidence in me.

My responsibility to my clients and my respect for the integrity of the agents with whom I worked became my "why." Making sure your clients' needs are met, one at a time—and they'll have many needs—will grow your confidence as a new agent. Make sure your word is your word. As you will hear in the real estate world, buyers and sellers come and go, but we agents will have one another to deal with for years. We need to be respectful of one another. It takes years to build a solid reputation and seconds to destroy it. Integrity is nonnegotiable.

As I'm sure you have noticed, money has not been mentioned. Money cannot be your power source or your "why," because it is not enough to feed you or your soul. While it is true that acquiring things costs money, what moves people powerfully through life is the feeling they experience when they achieve a goal. In *Think and Grow Rich,* Napoleon Hill quotes Andrew Carnegie, who says, "To succeed, you must love what you do." I've always loved what I do and "why" I do it.

A Day in Real Estate

Some of the appealing aspects of real estate are that it can work for different lifestyles and at various times in anyone's life. You could be a college student, a stay-at-home parent, or a divorcée. You could even be someone who has had a previous career and wants to reinvent yourself in the real estate profession. You can tailor your new career to your situation, which means you may work less or work more because of your life circumstances. The truth is there's room for everyone who has a desire to be in real estate. You never have to give up anything about your life in the pursuit of a real estate career. You can always be who you are and who you want to be.

The following two schedules are from two very different women working in real estate at different stages of their lives. Susan is a mom who needs to work from home because she has two young children. Kelly is a mother, but her children are grown, and she works primarily from her office. These schedules will give you an idea of how you could juggle your life obligations and have a real estate career as well.

SUSAN'S SCHEDULE

6:00 A.M.   Get up before kids, get dressed.
Eat while getting husband out the door for work.

7:00 A.M.   Get kids up, dressed, and fed.

8:00 A.M.   Check and return e-mails while kids play in the home office.

9:00 A.M.   Return phone calls and confirm appointments. Check the multiple listing service for new properties on the market. E-mail clients with possible homes to view.

10:45 A.M.   Drop kids off with babysitter and go to the gym.

12:00 P.M.   Go to the real estate office.

1:00 P.M.   Check in with the babysitter and organize showing schedule.

2:00 P.M.   Pick up client and show five houses.

3:30 P.M.   Drop client off at her home and head back to the office.

4:00 P.M.   Check e-mails and voice mails.

5:00 P.M.   Leave office for home.

6:30 P.M.   Prepare dinner.

7:00 P.M.   Dinner with family.

7:30 P.M.   Bath time for kids.

8:00 P.M.   Bedtime for kids.

11:00 P.M.   In bed.

KELLY'S SCHEDULE

6:30 A.M.   Get up, feed and take dogs out.

7:00 A.M.   Return e-mails and read *New York Times*, *New York Post,* and *LA Times.*

8:15 A.M.   Vigorous workout.

9:30 A.M.   Shower and get ready for work.

10:00 A.M.   Return calls and head to office.

11:00 A.M.   Take clients to see houses.

12:00 P.M.   Lunch in office, returning phone calls.

1:00 P.M.   Review contracts, marketing campaigns, and personal Web site.

2:30 P.M.   Negotiate offers and solve problems.

3:30 P.M.   Meet agents and their buyers at her listing.

4:30 P.M.   Return to office and meet with client to write
an offer.

6:00 P.M.   Call daughter and review the day's activities.

7:00 P.M.   Dinner with clients.

10:00 P.M. Map out next day's schedule,
let go of all the stress, and be grateful
for all the success.
Meditate and go to bed.

Think about it. Does your life fit into your real estate career, or does your real estate career fit into your life? The choice is yours!

Beginning Business Planning

Now you need to map out a schedule to provide continuity and organization and alleviate stress. Start with a daily schedule and expand it to a weekly one. Once you're comfortable with the routine, work your way up to a monthly plan and ultimately a yearly organizational chart. This is the beginning of goal setting, one step at a time.

Systematically approach your business as if you were your own client. Treat yourself kindly, be patient, be thorough, and be sure that you understand all facets of your plan. Then give it some pizzazz. Slowly make it more interesting by adding technological tools.

REFLECTIONS: MINDING YOUR BUSINESS

▶ Have a road map.

▶ Be organized.

▶ Use your time efficiently.

▶ Be consistent.

▶ Be informed about your marketplace.

▶ Be aware and informed about the business aspects of real estate.

▶ Reflect on your day and make notes of things left unfinished or things that could be improved.

▶ Be sure to plan your next day's schedule the day before.

Setting Boundaries

Lead, direct, and protect your clients. Real estate is a service-oriented business, and you are hired to provide the best in service and advice. Always be clear and honest when delivering the news. Don't avoid the tough questions. If your client asks a question that you can't answer, then research it and provide an intelligent answer. Don't volunteer information if you don't know it to be true. Always be honest with your client and work on establishing a relationship built on trust and respect. Remember your role as a real estate professional and act accordingly.

When I first began in real estate, there were no cell phones, so I gave everyone my home telephone number. If they didn't ask for it, I would offer it to them. Many times these were people I had just met at an open house, or brokers whom I wanted to get to know. I thought that by being available at all times, I would show how hard I was willing to work for people. Well, be careful what you wish for! My phone rang so much that I could barely finish one thing at home without being interrupted. I was so afraid to miss that one important call that I always answered the phone. The truth is that people don't respect you more when you're available 24/7. They will actually call you when they don't need anything. I found that many conversations were just to ask me if I knew certain information or (my favorite) if I could just look something up for them. The Internet did not exist at that time, so buyers and sellers relied on the real estate agent for up-to-date information on the market. The truth was that they really didn't need information at eleven at night. It took me several years to set boundaries and change the way I was working. My business actually improved when I took my home telephone number off of my voice mail recording. People then did business with me during business hours, and it gradually became a rarity that they needed to speak with me at night. Learning where my boundaries were gave me a more fulfilling personal and professional life.

Don't blur the lines of familiarity. I have represented

many friends over the years and have had to walk a fine line. I managed by setting out the rules from the start. Although we were friends, during the time we worked together as real estate agent and client, I still needed to lead them. I always maintained my composure and remained professional. As with any client, be 100 percent available during working hours. Set your hours according to your lifestyle, and when you end your day, turn off your phone. All work and no down time will diminish your ability to focus on your business. Be acutely aware of your limits and don't exceed them. Tired people make mistakes and say things they wish they hadn't. Listen to what your clients are saying and the questions they're asking and respond appropriately.

As real estate agents, time is our commodity. Once it's gone, it's lost to us forever. We have what I like to refer to as our "money hours." These hours are between 9:00 a.m. and 6:00 p.m. Monday through Friday and 10:00 a.m. to 5:00 p.m. on Saturday and Sunday. These hours are reserved for people who want to buy, sell, or lease real estate. When I first started out in real estate, I believed every person I met was a real buyer or seller. At first, I couldn't recognize the difference between those who wanted to transact a real estate deal and those who just wanted to occupy their time and mine. When I first started, we didn't prequalify buyers, and it was difficult to know how to read them. At times it seemed like people were looking at homes for the entertainment of it. Perhaps they were picking up decorating ideas and remodeling tips, but they were using my time at their leisure. When your time is your livelihood, you need to make your time work.

REFLECTIONS: STARTING OUT

▶ Listen to your clients.

▶ Establish a relationship built on trust and respect.

▶ Lead, direct, and protect your clients to the best of your ability.

▶ Be enthusiastic and positive.

▶ Be professional; don't get emotional.

▶ Be thorough and knowledgeable.

▶ Set boundaries.

▶ Be available during working hours.

▶ Don't blur the lines of familiarity.

Today we are able to prequalify a buyer, so this is less of a problem. I suggest to my newer agents that they create a relationship with their potential clients. They need to ask questions to understand their clients' needs and lifestyles. During this time they should ask them if they have a lender, and if not, they should refer them to a lender with whom they are familiar. If buyers are serious about purchasing a home, they will understand that prequalifying them financially is a natural part of the process. This also will give them credibility and affirm their purchasing power when they are ready to make an offer on a home.

In my business life, I had to learn to set boundaries and priorities, and so do you. Respecting yourself and your profession allows your clients to do the same. Our time is not free.

When I started I had two or three of the qualities that make a successful agent.

You will too!

Inspiration: Coach Ken

We've spent this chapter discussing the various aspects of what you, as a new agent, can expect when entering into real estate. There are moments when it can be stressful, as you have seen from my experiences. However, it is incredibly rewarding. I love my career. A big part of my success has been having people who are knowledgeable provide me with guidance. I've spent time working with different coaches and mentors. Today, I work with Ken Goodfellow at CKG International. He is a coach to top realtors and brokers worldwide, the 2005 Business Coach of the Year, and an entrepreneur, and he has twenty years' experience coaching in both the professional and sports industries. I have invited him to be interviewed for this book because I feel he has such valuable advice and has been so essential to my growth. I wanted to share his thoughts with you in his own powerful words so that they may inspire you too.

VALERIE: If you could give one piece of advice to someone starting out in the real estate industry, what would it be?

COACH KEN: Hire a coach, a mentor; start training immediately. With a coach, you will work on a business plan, know what you are working for, and set realistic goals. The training in real estate is varied, and you have to know where you want to concentrate your efforts. Work to get listings and buyers, learn scripts and dialogues, get on the telephone and prospect. What else do you have to do?

Remember, always follow up: There is a huge difference between saying you're going to do something and doing something.

VALERIE: Through your experience as both a professional coach and human being, what is the most valuable thing that you have learned about life?

COACH KEN: I've learned how much we are all the same and what it takes to stand out. We have the same fears, weaknesses, strengths, and aspirations. With some direction we can learn from other people's experiences and draw upon them to make ourselves stronger and more fulfilled.

VALERIE: I've talked a lot in this chapter about stress management. What tips can you give readers about

keeping stress in check? What about in the most difficult of moments?

COACH KEN: Perhaps the most helpful thing I've
learned about keeping stress in check is to identify
what I can control and what I can't control. I work
hard to control my working environment, my
thoughts, my goals, and my dreams. When I'm faced
with difficult decisions, I make my most educated decision and follow through. When things don't turn
out as I'd planned, I learn what I can and make a
better decision the next time.

For those most difficult moments I talk to someone I trust and respect, get a different perspective,
and make the decision to continue to work hard on
what I believe in. Again, controlling what I can and
letting the rest fall away is the best course.

VALERIE: A belief in yourself as a newly licensed real
estate agent is essential to both buyers and sellers.
What would you say is the most important part in
cultivating that confidence?

COACH KEN: To build my confidence I would remind
myself that I am a sum of all of my past experiences
and then draw from those experiences to realize that
even though I am newly licensed, my business experience is vast and I am bringing these strengths into
my new business. Working with a coach and learning

the essentials of the real estate business (listing presentation, time management, business planning, etc.) will cultivate the confidence to succeed and to succeed at a high level.

VALERIE: Managing your thoughts and beliefs is part of mental fitness. Can you tell me how to keep negative thoughts from derailing you from your goals and plans?

COACH KEN: Spend time every day learning about positive, successful people. Be inspired by the success of others and see yourself succeeding also. Through CKG coaching you can learn how other agents have started and been successful. By mirroring their activities and education you can succeed also.

VALERIE: Can you explain to our readers how coaching works?

COACH KEN: Coaching gives you a fast track to success. Your coach has worked with others who are in the same situation or at the same point in their business as you. Your coach has worked with tens or hundreds of agents experiencing the same levels of doubt, uncertainty, or expectation and can guide you from level to level with the most ease without you having to experience the hit or miss actions that so many others have to contend with.

VALERIE: From the coach's perspective, what can a newly licensed agent expect to gain from the coaching process?

COACH KEN: A newly licensed agent who makes the decision to hire a coach has committed to the business and committed to himself to be successful. The confidence gained from having a business plan and learning how to execute each point in the plan guarantees success.

A coach will guide you through those uncertain first months where so much time is wasted "wondering what I should be doing." Instead, it will give the agent a definite time management plan, schedule, sales training, and assurance that this is one of the most lucrative businesses in which to be involved.

VALERIE: In closing, what words of inspiration would you like to leave with our readers?

COACH KEN: As you embark on a new career in real estate or make the decision to begin to treat your real estate business as a lucrative, profitable career, take a hard, long look at your goals, skills, and the education available to you. Understand that you'll be rewarded for working hard, but that working smarter has to be your path to financial and personal success. Be excited every day about what you do or find another job. Your excitement will lead you to excellence—search for the best or a better way. Remember, life is a learning experience. Employ mentors and coaches and surround yourself with people who will help you achieve your goals. As you can see, you need to show up physically, emotionally, and mentally to be successful in real estate. Your next step is to get organized, have a schedule, and master your time.

Attitudes are not positive or negative
until you make a decision to go for a goal.

—LOU TICE

CHAPTER FOUR

You Become What You Believe

Y ou can do so much more than you can imagine in real estate if you're organized. As you begin to map out a schedule that works for you, you'll realize that there are so many things that you need to get done every day. But once you master your time and your mind, the results that you'll enjoy are unlimited.

Multitasking

Multitasking is a skill that is important for you to learn. There are only so many hours in a day. You have a finite amount of energy and an infinite number of tasks to accomplish and dreams to fulfill.

I want you take a pen and paper and make a chart of

what you did for the last week from the time you woke up until you got into bed. When you've finished, I want you to look over your list of activities very carefully. Where did you spend your time? Was there one activity where you spent more time, either because you were obligated to or because you enjoyed it? Do you participate in family activities every day? Do you go to the gym three times a week? Do you currently have a job that you would need to continue while you get going in your real estate career? Is there any time left in a day to purposefully pursue your real estate career? Are you willing to rearrange your current priorities to make a larger space for your real estate career? Does your career rise to the top of your list or fall somewhere in the middle?

There is a time and a place for everything in your life. There may be times when you'll be concentrating on your personal life, professional life, family life, or educational pursuits. However, all facets of your life will eventually come together to create the whole you. When I meet with new agents, I always ask them the same question, and rarely do they have an immediate answer. I'll pose the question to you now. Do you see your life fitting into your real estate career or your real estate career fitting into your life? When you can honestly answer this question, your priorities and goals will become clear. For many of us who are already on the career path, this is a good question to help us reevaluate our goals. Making adjustments in your priorities and goals can be just like last-minute changes that occur in a day of penciled-in appointments. There are many forks in our real estate career road. Sometimes we veer to the left or the right or down a new path that takes us on an adventure.

Whatever your path, try not to lose sight of the big picture. I learned this the hard way. When I first started out in real estate, I worked for three years and nine months without taking a single day off. I was actually scared to. I was scared that if I stopped, the momentum would fall apart and I would lose it all. I mistakenly thought that people wouldn't want to work with me if they couldn't reach me every minute. I believed that I could easily be replaced and that my current prospects would find somebody else to help them buy or sell a home. Yet so much time went by without me taking care of myself that I forgot how to rest. Some old habits die hard, they say. Even to this day I find myself going long periods of time without taking a break.

There were times that I was running like crazy just to fit so many things into my day. One experience at my daughter's school made me stop dead in my tracks and reflect on the effect that my behavior was having on my little girl. I can remember going to Vanessa's first-grade parent night, and I was the only single parent there, which made me feel as though I stood out and was different from the other parents. That evening the classroom was filled with drawings that the children had made of their families. The children's assignment was to write about when they were the most happy. Next to Vanessa's picture she wrote in big block letters, the way young children write, "I AM HAPPY WHEN MY MOMMY DOES NOT WORK ALL DAY ON SATURDAY. I AM HAPPY WHEN MY MOMMY IS NOT YELLING ON THE PHONE."

That experience was an "ah-ha" moment for me. It was clearly time for me to reflect on my multitasking and the amount of time I was giving to my business and the effect it was having on my daughter. That evening at her school, I decided to take time off and take her away on a trip. From that moment on, I was going to try to make an effort to be more balanced about my life.

Planning helps you manage a busy schedule. It is the tool with which you can accomplish everything. Planning comes naturally; you do it without even thinking about it. In fact, in many situations you look forward to it. Think of things you plan each year: birthday parties, holiday dinners, vacations, and all sorts of celebrations. You will find it is similar to creating a business calendar and a business plan. A business calendar is a calendar outlining your day. A business plan is an outline of the goals to accomplish to ensure the success of your business. With a positive attitude, every day can be a wonderful new and exciting learning experience. To keep your life balanced, you must be strong, present, and accountable.

Life is a delicate balance, and it is especially challenging for people who have children or family members who need them. Take the time now as you embark on your real estate career to have patience, compassion, and understanding, and keep in mind that there is a time and a place for everything.

Blind Faith

It's important to move purposefully forward to achieve your objective. Believe that you can make your dreams come true. This is one of the most important lessons and one that separates the superachievers from the crowd. Belief systems drive your mind and direct your heart. Remember, you are what you believe.

Early on, after I started making a sale here and there, I met a man who had a profound effect on my life. I was still struggling when this opportunity fell in my lap. A friend and the successful CEO of a real estate company offered me a ticket to a seminar taught by Lou Tice, chairman of the Pacific Institute and a widely respected featured speaker for many Fortune 1000 companies. I bought an airline ticket that I couldn't really afford but knew would pay off and headed to the seminar. Gathered there were fifty CEOs from major companies nationwide—and me. I was so excited to be there and wanted so badly to be in that crowd, not for the prestige, but for the knowledge.

I had the double honor of being the only woman and the only person there who wasn't a wealthy CEO. I was broke at the time, but I was the only one who knew it. I held my head high and pretended to fit in. I remember being so nervous that someone would discover that I didn't belong there. I reflected on Vanessa, knew she was in good hands with my trusted neighbor, and determined to get the most out of this seminar. Lou put on music and had us write down our hopes and dreams for our lives and businesses.

He told us to make it big, make it huge, make it materialistic. What would we do if nothing held us back? As if I were back in high school, I leaned over my desk, covering my paper with my hand so no one could see my answers. I was so embarrassed. I wrote down that I wanted to make $1 million and have a beach house.

Lou gave us the task of reading what we had written aloud every night before bed. He said that we are what we believe and we become what we hold to be true. I wasn't really convinced that this exercise would mean anything, but he was the expert. For the next six months, my business grew steadily. Within one year I had made $1 million and had a beach house. Well, half of a beach house—a rental for the summer months. Lou Tice taught me the value of believing in myself. He was the man who taught me empowerment through positive thought, and by taking small steps, just how quickly I could change the direction of my life.

I made the decision to trust to blind faith. I didn't know how I would do it, but I knew where I was going—straight to the top! Empty Rolodex and all, I was determined to make it. There were things I knew I didn't want to do when I first began my real estate business, so I hired an assistant. I didn't know how to lead her, but I knew what things needed to get done. So when she asked me what she should do, I gave her a list of all the things that I didn't want to do and told her to do them. In what seemed like a stroke of genius, I came up with my first business plan. I decided that I needed to pay an assistant, even though this meant that I couldn't pay my taxes. Yes, it's true, every cause has an effect and every choice has a consequence. This was maybe not my most intelligent decision, but it seemed like a good idea at the time. I decided that my taxes could wait, which would have its consequences at a later date.

Very few agents at that time had assistants. Everyone thought I was crazy. Today I have an administrative staff of five with eight junior agents working with me. I have a long client list. I still keep my old Rolodex on my desk to remind me how far I've come and how far I still have to go.

Ambition

I had to have the will to be brave and act boldly so my dreams would mirror my beliefs. I had to be resilient even when I foresaw and actually experienced many obstacles and setbacks. Prior to meeting Lou Tice, I would just put a dream out there without a clue of how to reach it. I learned from him how to focus on, believe in, and drive my dreams.

Your natural way of being and responding are direct results of the way you grew up and the environment that surrounded you. How you think and feel, expressions that you use, and habits that you repeat have shaped your character and your outlook on life. You need to keep your beliefs as positive as possible, even through trying events such as divorce, the death of a loved one, financial setbacks, or family health issues. I have experienced each of these situations and fought the monkey on my shoulder every time. I contained my negative thoughts and feelings in a box, and have continued to do so until today.

What if it doesn't work?

They won't listen to me.

What if I'm wrong?

I figured that if those thoughts and feelings were safely away from me, I could move forward faster. It was important to set aside my doubts and not to give them attention or power. When you really want to change your life, you will find the strength and passion to do just that. If you really want something, signs of what you want will begin to pop up everywhere in your life. Your awareness is the first step to embarking on a path to discover how to get what you want. At this moment, by reading this book, you are at the awareness stage, the first step toward making a positive change in your life.

When you are fearful, ask yourself what it is that makes you uncomfortable. For many years, I would attend conferences around the country and agents would ask me how to sell a million-dollar house. I would always ask them what the average price of a home was in their local area. A woman named Mary told me that she sold houses in Louisville, Kentucky, my mother's hometown. She told me that the average sales price was $125,000 and that she typically sold 325 homes per year. I was stunned that she was asking me how to be a successful agent when I was selling only seven or eight homes at that time. Even though some of my homes were well over $1 million, in my eyes, Mary was a more successful agent than I. I looked at her with admiration and could barely contain my embarrassment that she was asking me for advice. Yet, in Mary's eyes, I was more accomplished.

Many times we look at someone else and say to ourselves that they are smarter, luckier, and more successful than we are and we ask ourselves why we can't be more like them. The truth is you can't measure yourself by anyone else's accomplishments or standards. You can only measure yourself to your own accomplishments. The question is, are you successful to yourself? Whatever that means to you, you should celebrate it.

I was so amazed by the idea that Mary could possibly sell 325 homes per year. The sheer thought of having to talk to that many people, negotiating the price, doing all that paperwork, and closing those sales seemed incomprehensible. Likewise, Mary was so impressed that I could represent homes that could be worth $1 million and she believed there was something magical about that.

What we learned that day was the profound respect we

had for the way each of us ran our business. This is a lesson I keep with me every day of my life. I admire people who do things from which I can learn.

Thinking Big

Thinking big involves risk and usually does not meet the approval of others. It is marching to the beat of your own heart and soul; it is doing what feels right to you. When you take a leap of blind faith and put your energy behind your dreams, a combination of feelings rises to the surface. You may feel so invincible you could fly and at the same time feel so nervous that you can't move your feet. There are no guarantees in life, and as the old adage goes, "Nothing ventured, nothing gained." You'll never know unless you try. Don't be attached to an outcome; be committed to your dream. There is a difference, and that difference lies in you.

Only you can fully feel the impact of your desires. You can explain them to others, but they can only hear the plan and guess at the outcome. Looking outside for confirmation can sometimes be an obstacle in accomplishing your dream. It's vital to have confidence in yourself.

When I said, "Who, me?" to the idea of being a successful entrepreneur, it came from my discomfort and lack of faith in myself and my talent. Although others began to recognize my efforts and promising career path, it was meaningless until I believed in myself. It wasn't until I developed habits, beliefs, and attitudes that gave me the courage to think big and the conviction to make my dreams come true that I began to feel truly successful.

It seemed at a certain point that my choices were working for me. I had hired an assistant early on in my real estate practice. I was multitasking a million things at the same time and seemed to be keeping up with most of them. My daughter was doing well and was in a school she loved, and I was attending all of her dance recitals. I sought out advice and help to learn how to grow my business. I was getting back my old self-confidence and found myself laughing more. All of a sudden it dawned on me: I was trusting myself to make decisions, and those decisions were turning out well. My thinking had become bigger, and I was experiencing the feeling of letting go and trusting my intuition and decision making.

Maybe one of your greatest strengths is difficult to measure or to put into words. Maybe your talent is like mine—interacting with people and having a positive attitude. The ability to connect with others is immeasurably important in terms of the happiness it will bring you and those with whom you come into contact. In many ways you hold the key to unlocking your clients' hopes and dreams.

Think big and think simply. What is it that you really want? Don't force a feeling or pursue a career in a certain field just to please others or because you feel that it's what's expected of you. You have to do what brings you joy. Surrendering your path in life only breeds poverty of mind and soul. The bigger you think, the easier it will be to decide if it's the correct path or career for you. That's not to imply that you won't have to work hard, it just means that when it's right, you'll know it. You can feel it. You chose to read this book, so perhaps it feels right for you to pursue a career in real estate. You can imagine yourself successfully representing buyers and sellers, making their dreams and yours come true. The idea of a real estate career puts a smile on your face. I bet you're smiling right now!

Rewards

One time I was working as the buyers' agent for a young, newly married Orthodox Jewish couple who were in the market to buy their first home. He wanted to be able to walk to his parents' home. She wanted to live in a young and trendy area in the hills, away from his parents and in line with the lifestyle she enjoyed in San Francisco, where they had met. As newlyweds, deciding where to live was a point of contention. She viewed his neighborhood choice as old-fashioned and too traditional for her taste. He viewed her neighborhood choice as an impractical place to begin a family.

As we began developing a relationship, I learned that Liza had previously run her own business from her home and planned on doing so in Los Angeles. Being in a trendy neighborhood was inspiring for her. Even though she was ready to start a family, she feared that living in any other type of neighborhood would compromise her creative edge. She wanted to be in a modern setting with the convenience of lots of nearby restaurants, book stores, and entertainment. Joseph enjoyed these things as well but valued having his family close by and was focused on the needs that come with beginning a family. He wanted to honor both his family and his religious traditions.

As the mother of a toddler at the time, I knew how valuable having a support system close by would be. It was my job to show them homes, which was going to be very challenging. It was important to me to see them happy and in agreement. Beginning a life together is an exciting time in a couple's life. However, when you consider the emotional roller coaster involved in buying a first home, and add two people who want completely different lifestyles, well . . . newlywed bliss sometimes isn't so blissful.

We began to discuss the lifestyle that comes with becoming new parents. When Liza and Joseph spoke of starting a family, you could see their eyes light up and the loving bond they shared. I took them to view several homes in both areas, explaining the benefits and possible concerns of each: the schools, parks, noise levels, traffic, etc. We drove through and around both neighborhoods each time we looked at homes. As time passed, Liza began to notice the families on the sidewalks in the area Joseph loved. The parks were full of children, and there was also much less traffic and nighttime noise. The many conveniences available in the area where Joseph wanted to live greatly exceeded those in the trendy areas Liza originally favored. As time went by, Joseph's neighborhood began to sell itself.

Liza's reluctance began to dissolve. She began to see Joseph's neighborhood favorably for the first time, and they ended up buying a house there. Liza and Joseph are happily married now and have two children, playing in those very parks I had taken the couple to see.

Showing homes to couples can be challenging when they have dramatically different tastes from each other. When working with couples, you need to hear both of their concerns and make each person feel acknowledged by showing them what they each want, even if they want different things. Show them the homes they have described to you. By doing this, you will be letting them explore their thoughts and ideas of what they want in their new home. This process will give them enough time to see properties together and come to a mutual agreement on their own. You will also allow them to find their own way and feel satisfied because in the end, they are selecting their home themselves. Buyers really want the experience of finding their home rather than being sold on a home.

There are few moments in real estate that are as fulfilling and emotionally rewarding as helping a young couple accomplish the dream of buying their first home. When you experience the satisfaction of this moment you will understand exactly what I mean!

Attitude

There is no room for indifference. You must choose an attitude and take a position. To be successful you have to make a commitment to a goal. A positive attitude allows you to look forward eagerly to things in your day while still appreciating the present moment. Enthusiastically plan your daily activities, whether it's walking, exercising, eating healthy, reading, working, or spending quality time with your family. Always look forward to your tasks by making them interesting and positive. Even if something is difficult, see it as a challenge and an opportunity to grow. Small steps are so important. All it takes is a slight adjustment and your picture can change 180 degrees.

Don't dwell on uncomfortable things that happened in the past. Keep in mind that we have all had trying experiences to varying degrees in our lives. Move on to the present and the future. Like a golfer who executed a poor shot to the green or a tennis player who double-faulted a serve, you must forget about those temporary setbacks and concentrate on the now. The mind is a powerful tool, and it's important to keep thinking positive thoughts.

Don't worry about what might happen. You don't have a crystal ball and can't predict the future. Worrying about things that haven't happened yet will negatively affect your energy and outlook. Your real estate business will be driven by your attitude. If you keep your attention on the deal at hand and the client in front of you, your clients will feel well taken care of by the knowledge and support you share with them.

What you think about yourself determines your self-worth. Every day you will be expected to determine worth of some kind. How much is this house worth? You'll hear it time and again. How can you determine the value of anything if you don't know your own self-worth? A confident person speaks with conviction and passion. Speak the truth as you know it, and believe it to be so. You must keep your emotions in check. Many times you will need to hold your tongue and bite your lip. As you know, I learned that lesson the hard way early on in my career when I hung up on agents and clients who were yelling at me. As a result, I didn't sell a property for nine months. You can't take things personally as I did at that time. Remember, it's just the news.

Get up every morning and feel like a million dollars and chances are you'll go out there and make a million dollars. Feel like a winner and you'll be one. Feel like a leader and you'll assume your position as a trusted advisor, a knowledgeable negotiator, and a responsible real estate agent. You will lead your clients through the twists and turns of the transaction and the ups and downs of your marketplace. There will undoubtedly be some of those. So be prepared.

Belief Systems and a Goal-Setting Lifestyle

As you make changes in your life, the old you shows up less frequently. Remember the drama queen that I was, hanging up on people and smelling dead rats in my closet? Eventually those old ways of behaving fall by the wayside. You'll find yourself talking and dealing with people in a different way. As you grow, all the changes that you make will disturb the old idea that your friends and family previously had of you.

As the new you emerges, new people will come into your life. Often they will try to test your boundaries. When I first started out in real estate, there was a hugely successful woman in my marketplace. It seemed as though every time I met someone who was interested in buying or selling a home, she would find out about it. She would call me and insist that since she knew them she was entitled to 50 percent of any business I transacted with them. I felt suffocated and controlled. I also felt scared because she was far more established in the real estate business than I was, but I knew I had to take a stand. I evaluated my options, and I decided that I wanted to build my own reputation in real estate and not be forced into an unfair partnering relationship. Splitting commissions is a normal part of transactions. There is, however, a proper way to split commissions with brokers, as opposed to being bullied. So what are you to do when faced with what you believe is an unjust situation between you and another agent or broker? You go to arbitration.

Arbitration is a conflict-resolution process where you take your complaint before a board of your peers in the real estate industry. Over a period of ten years, I took the same person before the board three times. At first I was afraid to take action, but it was important to me to stand up for my beliefs. Standing up for your beliefs will establish your reputation in your business community.

You have an incredible opportunity now to break free of all those uncomfortable situations and old, unprofitable comfort zones financially, emotionally, and personally. You can free yourself to try new adventures. Once I tried race-car driving. You could try skydiving, or you could muster the spirit to stick your toe into the real estate waters. Before you know it, you'll be swimming the backstroke in the deep end.

Ask yourself if you have any core beliefs or fears that would hold you back. Do you believe that you're not smart enough, not educated enough, technologically challenged? How can you dramatically alter your life to change your path and reach your goal? Is your present environment not conducive to growth or change? Do you have money concerns? What is stopping you from taking a chance on yourself? How would you dramatically alter your life if you chose to do so?

All thoughts and actions have energy. Allow yourself to dream about what you want. Don't worry if you're not qualified. Often buyers feel a sense of accomplishment when buying a nicer home. They aspire to have bigger homes and live in more desirable neighborhoods. Do you have similar aspirations? How will you get where you're going? You will lead the way, of course!

In order to set goals, there are important questions to ask yourself. The following list will give you plenty to reflect upon. Be honest. Only you will know if your answers are true for you.

- ▶ I look forward to accomplishing_____today.

- ▶ I intend to_____.

- ▶ My first step will be_____.

▶ I can see myself doing_____.

▶ I want to give up_____attitude.

▶ I want to give up_____emotion because it no longer is working in my life.

▶ To accomplish my goals, I will no longer avoid_____.

▶ Are my feelings and actions often at odds with each other?

▶ Am I concerned with how others see me or how I see myself?

Leadership

Webster's dictionary describes a leader as one who shows the way, guides in direction. Except for playing the Pied Piper to Vanessa and my neighbor's children, I never had had to lead before, but I believed that I could. In chapter 1, I described a moment in my life when I failed to recognize myself as others saw me, as a successful businesswoman and entrepreneur. I clearly remember saying aloud, "Who, me?" That was an "ah-ha" moment for me. I realized that the tremendous amount of hard work and effort that I had been putting into my professional life was being recognized by others as leadership. I had never thought of myself as a leader. I guess, in my eyes, I didn't fit the definition because my perception of a leader was a hard, cold, tough person, but I was wrong.

We are born into this world led by a doctor's hands. We are led by parents who show us how to walk, talk, laugh, sing, and play. We are led by teachers who teach us to think, to write, to read, and to create. For the majority of our young lives, we are pretty much directed, instructed, guided, and led by the hand. Then one day, the leaders are gone and we have to figure out a way to become our own leader. We need to learn to handle responsibility, make decisions, and live with our choices, which will surely cause us either to fail or to succeed. Every decision matters and has a consequence.

Leadership is one of the most important skills you will acquire as a real estate agent. In almost every speech I have given at conferences across the country, I have mentioned our role as leaders. We lead our buyers and sellers through some of the most important decisions they will ever make. We lead them whether it involves the sale or purchase of a property. Buyers and sellers could be making decisions during unfortunate circumstances involving a death or divorce, or happier occasions such as a new addition to a growing family, or a recent marriage. People sell their big homes to purchase smaller ones when they become empty nesters. They sell smaller properties to purchase larger ones when they have more money. Whatever the case, it is our job to lead our buyers and sellers by understanding their issues and fulfilling their real estate needs at any given moment.

To be a strong leader, you need to have complete knowledge of your local marketplace. It is vitally important that your clients see you as their leader and have faith in your abilities and decision-making capabilities so that they will feel protected. It is equally important that your fellow agents have faith in your abilities and see you as a cooperative working partner and co-leader in a transaction.

Believe that what drives you is the desire to do your job well and offer your clients the very best in guidance and customer service. Never come from a place of greed or ego. Know that what sustains you and makes you unique in your field is your pursuit of excellence and your willingness to put your clients' needs before your own. Try to always do your best and don't be afraid to make a mistake. You are human, after all. If you make a mistake, don't try to cover it up. Simply acknowledge the situation, do what you can to rectify it, and move on. Your clients will appreciate your sincerity. Know that the direction in which you are leading is a path worthy of the journey. Good leaders take people with them toward their goals. If you lead with excitement, passion, and sincerity others will happily follow in your footsteps. If you enjoy what you do and believe in what you are conveying, your words will ring true not only for you but for those whom you lead.

SEVEN LEADERSHIP MYTHS

1. To be a leader you have to be rough, tough, and firm.

2. Leadership means you are always right.

3. Taking the lead is grabbing it from someone else.

4. As a leader you will worry all the time.

5. Leaders are born, not made.

6. Leaders are in control all the time.

7. Leaders are always self-motivated.

SEVEN LEADERSHIP REALITIES

1. Leaders are secure and are able to lead with ease.

2. Leaders are open to suggestions and are willing to learn from others.

3. Leaders take the responsibility of leading without infringing on the rights of others.

4. Leaders are prepared and make decisions that are well thought out and researched.

5. Leaders often learn how to lead during times of adversity.

6. Leaders have a strong work ethic and are not afraid to be flexible when appropriate.

7. Leaders are often motivated by new ideas they've learned from others.

Teamwork

The process may differ from state to state, but the core group of players in a real estate deal remains the same. There are the agents for the buyer and seller, the inspectors who come to test the systems of the house, the lenders who supply the money, and of course the buyer and the seller. In the Los Angeles area there are a host of additional inspectors, looking down chimneys, climbing on roofs, snaking cameras through sewer lines, climbing up and down hillsides. There are appraisers measuring rooms and comparing prices in the area. There are title representatives providing deed information, and third parties called escrow officers who are in charge of processing mounds of required documents. As the agent on one side of a transaction, you must help lead this team of professionals through the entire process. Your primary responsibility and accountability will always be to your clients. In chapter 3 we talked about being prepared. This is important to keep your stress level at a minimum, make the clients feel at ease, and let them know they are in good hands. Be familiar with the required paperwork, inside and out. Don't put yourself in front of a client without being able to explain every clause of a contract, which will help your clients through the process of buying and selling. With your familiarity with contracts, you will be able to speak with an air of authority and confidence. Always be the leader, but remember that throughout this process, you are part of a team.

I learned a valuable lesson that has stuck with me for many years. I was on the phone explaining to the buyer what

HE had to do. I kept telling him over and over that HE had to do this and HE had to do that. Finally, he lost his temper and screamed into the phone that HE didn't have to do anything, including work with me! At that moment I realized how isolating it must have felt to him when I told him what HE had to do. I should have said what WE had to do. After all, WE were working as a team. Ever since that time, whenever speaking with clients and giving my advice, I use WE.

Don't cross the line personally. Maintain a professional boundary at all times. Your clients may attempt to engage you in conversations that make you privy to their personal situations. There will be times when it will seem like you are a psychologist, an attorney, or an accountant. Clients may seek advice on detailed financial or legal matters. Many people lose their sense of reason and ability to communicate sensibly when it comes to their money. Even friends can become unrecognizable and unreasonable during the buying and selling process, but it's your job to steer the situation toward a positive outcome. You do that by remaining in control. Don't let it get personal.

Early in my career I met and became very good friends with a woman whom I'll call Joan. We met through mutual friends. We shared the same hair stylist, and every Valentine's Day we'd have lunch, exchange presents, and toast ourselves. I didn't have anyone to share this day with, and her husband was usually away on business. We also created our own holidays, talked about our children, and had plenty of laughs.

We were friends for about five years when she shared with me that she and her husband were getting a divorce.

She wanted to move out of their home and buy her own place. She asked me to help her, and of course I did. I thought we knew each other well enough that she'd trust my direction and my advice. Well, she went from wanting my leadership to questioning my motivations. I went from laughing with her to being screamed at by her. Our friendship began to unravel.

I was so inexperienced at the time that I didn't know how to manage the situation and I didn't know how to save our friendship. I took her fear and nervousness personally. I didn't know how to step back from the emotional aspect of our friendship. I wanted to alleviate her anxiety, but instead I seemed to add to it, maybe because I wanted so much to make it right. During this time, our friendship lost its meaning and we lost faith in each other. We need to feel safe in our friendships for them to flourish. I am still sad about the loss of that friendship.

It's often said that "it's not what happens to you but how you react to it." Looking back on that unfortunate situation with my friend, I have to take ownership of my behavior. I should not have allowed myself to get as emotionally involved as I did. Since that experience, I have never reacted in that manner again. I am very careful to monitor myself when representing people close to me, so I don't allow myself to get swept up in the moment of helping them, taking the chance of losing my composure. As you can see, by losing my composure, I added to my friend's stress level. If I had kept a cool head, I would have been able to help her in a different and better way.

Teamwork is essential in the real estate business. Establish a strong working relationship with clients and agents representing the other parties in your real estate transactions. This is not an adversarial relationship. You should be working together toward the same goal on behalf of the buyers and sellers you both are representing. You need internal strength and sometimes external support to be successful.

One of the most famous examples of teamwork is the story of Rocky Balboa. Rocky had the internal strength to fight, and having his team behind him helped him to achieve his goal. He was down, but he stayed in the game. He knew the challenge before him and he needed professional advice and guidance to make it happen. Rocky had the heart that made his dreams possible, and with his team working together, nothing was impossible. First he got himself into shape by running through Philadelphia in the cold and the rain, sparring, working out, and eating raw eggs. He was relentless in his pursuit of accomplishing his goal. He had a system, he had support, and he had blind faith in himself.

Just as Rocky had the ability to stay focused and determined to win and be the best, you undoubtedly have these qualities too.

To be successful in business you need to contain the monkey on your shoulder, strive to be in a good place emotionally, and be well organized. These facets are all linked in the real estate business. You need to create a strong foundation upon which to build your business. See the big picture and know how hard it is to get from one point to another, but understand that all you really need to know is how to start. I have consistently listened and made changes in my business plan as I was growing. As I grew, my business grew. My organizational systems have become more sophisticated. I've moved from a working space in my small apartment, to a desk in an office, to a tiny windowless office, to an entire suite of offices. I did it step by step, and you can too.

It is not the mountain we conquer
but ourselves.

—SIR EDMUND HILLARY

CHAPTER FIVE

Finding Your Way

O nce you have established the company with which you'll be affiliated, you will need guidance from the office manager. Managers are fully aware that new real estate licensees need training in every aspect of the real estate business. They will be happy to share their experience and time with you. You are an investment in the office's potential overall production and achievement. When a manager hires you, she believes that you have what it takes to be an asset to the office and a success in real estate. This is the time to show your new manager your enthusiasm, positive energy, and willingness to learn and work hard. By this time, you know that real estate agents work on commission and only get paid when they close a transaction. It's important to jump in with both feet to learn as much as you can as quickly as you can. Ask about available training programs in the office. The success of your real estate career will be a direct result of the amount of time and energy you put into it. It's largely up to you how many hours of training you sign up for. Your office may have minimum requirements, but I would suggest attending as many training sessions as possible. Remember, I learned a great deal from listening to and learning from the more seasoned agents around me.

This is the time and place you begin developing your skills. Think of your manager as your first mentor. As your mentor, one of your manager's jobs is to help you attain your dreams and reach your goals efficiently and effectively. Your manager can guide you down the many paths you will need to navigate and help you choose the right one to lead you to a successful real estate career. Good managers will also hold you accountable for working toward the goals you've set for yourself.

Organizing Your Office

Whether you work from home or in the office, you need to find a space where you can be organized. Even if you don't have a desk in the office or you work from a table in your home, your work space must put you in a work mode. So much of this business, like life, is feeling the part. If you're working from home and don't have a desk space, identify an area where you can sit quietly and focus, without distractions. From now on, that is your work space. You need to feel like you're going to work. If you have a desk in your home, clear off anything that's on it now. It's important to see the space as your real estate desk. Things that you'll need on your desk include paper, pens, files, computer, and perhaps an old Rolodex that you will replace with a new computer database or contact list. Create separate boxes or folders that will hold things that need immediate attention, another for things to follow up on, and perhaps one for ideas of new things that you would like to accomplish.

Once you begin to develop a client list of buyers and sellers, you'll need to have a system to keep their contact information and paperwork organized. The way you follow up on your prospects should be the same whether you work from home or in a real estate office. If you join an office as a new licensee, you may have to share a desk with another new licensee, or perhaps you might be fortunate enough to have a desk of your own. Most companies have specific policies regarding desk space. Usually, the new agents and less productive agents share a desk in the bull pen area, a group of cubicles in the center of the office. It's less private, more open. It's actually a good place to listen and learn. This is the same style of business management used by most employers of independent contractors. Very rarely will a new agent have a private office. If you have the opportunity to see your physical space before officially joining the office, you should seriously consider if you're able to work in that environment. No matter where it is, every time you sit down in your chair, your focus should turn to real estate.

Whatever happened before you walked into the office needs to stay outside the office. You must be disciplined and positive. Discipline, consistency, and a positive attitude help you stick to your commitments. Discipline comes from within the mind and the heart. Begin a system and organize different folders, label and alphabetize them in different drawers for buyers and sellers. Even if you don't have any clients right now, prepare your systems anyway. In addition, create a folder for your education efforts and another for every important real estate form. Some states, like California, have contract forms online. It's critical to learn the forms. Be diligent about attending office meetings and keep current on all legal updates. If you don't understand the purpose of a specific form or the legal language employed, make sure that you ask and get clarification from your manager or training director.

REFLECTIONS: GETTING ORGANIZED

▶ Envision your work area.

▶ Decide if you would prefer to work from home or an office.

▶ Make sure that your space is as private as possible so you can concentrate on what you're doing.

▶ Make a commitment to how many days a week you will work and stick to it.

Prospecting

It all starts with baby steps. Have a daily routine and stick to it. Are you ready to get to work? Are you sitting at your work space? Who are your clients? They're out there, but they won't find you, you have to find them. How do you do that? Who do you know who might want to buy or sell a property? Do you have a database? What is a database?

The single most important thing you can do as a real estate professional is to take the time to sit down and make a list of everyone you know. This will become your database. They may be doctors, neighbors, religious organizations, children's school or play groups, volunteer organizations, your dry cleaner, dentist, and car mechanic—virtually anyone with whom you come into contact in your life. Since many of you have had previous jobs or careers before entering into real estate, don't forget about those contacts too! Even your parents and relatives have phone books of people they have known throughout their lives that could be a valuable resource for you.

Keep in mind that everyone on your list will know other people as well. Your database has now become full of potential prospects whom you can begin to mail, e-mail, and call with real estate information. People love to hear about real estate. They love to hear about what's going on in their neighborhood, who's selling and for what price, what sold, and what opportunities there are to purchase property. Believe me, everyone loves to know a person in real estate, and now that person is you!

The new agents who want to work with me usually come into my office and sheepishly say they really don't know many people. But unless they have just moved into the area, they are surprised to realize how many people they actually do know, once we talk about their hobbies, interests, family, education, and previous experiences.

When you have a list of all of your contacts, you're ready to begin your business by sending out a mailing to let them know that you're now in real estate. Make a seven-day calendar to begin with and list when you'll do your mailing, when you'll follow up with a call, and when you might send them an e-mail. That way you can track your contact with them. Understand that with this important exercise you are getting your real estate career off to a great start. There are many seasoned agents who have never set up a database. By doing so, you will forge ahead of them!

Now you need to get the word out and be prepared to do business intelligently. That means don't make a call if you don't have any idea of what you're going to say. When you ask questions, make sure you have a pen and paper to take down the responses. Everything should be planned ahead of time. Begin by calling the people whom you know best. Once you have a scheduled system, how many calls and e-mails will you commit to making each day?

REFLECTIONS: MAKING CONTACT

▶ List the first five people whom you'll call to tell them you're in real estate.

▶ Include everyone you know and meet in your database of people to contact.

▶ Make a plan of how many calls and e-mails you will make each day and stick to it.

Dialogue for Phone Calls and E-mail Content

One of your most important tools will be your communication skills. How are you going to keep the conversation going? What will you say? You're calling for a reason. You want their business or their referrals to other people. You should be positive, affirmative, and not too aggressive or demanding. Make sure that you have a working knowledge of the local real estate inventory and ideas for the people to whom you speak. If you're calling people you know well, you may have an idea of what they want. However, don't assume that you have the answers. Ask questions, listen, and take notes on everything from their personal information to their real estate needs. Some discussions may be about their children, their jobs, or their new lives. Next time you call, you'll remember more about them. This is called warm calling. If you feel that it will be helpful to you, transfer the information you learn from your call into your contact database.

Another idea would be to e-mail friends and family. E-mail is an excellent noninvasive way to keep the lines of communication open within your contact base. No matter how close you are with a person, sometimes this approach works better. No one is in the mood to talk all the time. If you use a day planner, a computer, or perhaps a smart phone, make sure to keep track of when you e-mailed or called your prospects. Note the highlights of your conversation and when it would be a good time to call again. Set a schedule. After you feel comfortable with calling people you know, you can try cold calling and door knocking. Cold calling is phoning prospective buyers and sellers whom you don't know. Door knocking is going to properties and introducing yourself in person. It will be important to get business cards with your contact information and maybe even a photo on them. Hand them out everywhere—at the grocery store, when you go to the dentist or the doctor, anyplace you meet people. Eventually, people will begin to put your face and your name together.

I had been a real estate agent for at least four or five years when I attended a seminar that focused heavily on cold calling, door knocking, and neuro-linguistic programming (NLP), which really means modulating the tone and intonation with which you speak. I was excited about everything I learned from this program, and I felt energized and motivated to use my new set of skills to reach my goals.

According to what I had heard and learned at this seminar, the most effective time of day to speak with prospects was in the morning before they left for work. Furthermore, the best way to express my enthusiasm and connect with them was speaking to them while standing up the entire time. My understanding was that it would infuse positive energy into my voice and project a more engaging demeanor. Goodness knows that under my circumstances, I needed all the help I could get. Every weekday morning I awoke at six o'clock to get ready to go to my real estate office, as I simultaneously juggled getting Vanessa fed and dressed. I arranged for my neighbor to take the early morning child-care shift so I could be sitting at my desk by seven-thirty. Well, actually, I wasn't sitting, I was standing. I diligently performed this morning ritual every day, even though it broke my heart when Vanessa cried, hanging on to me, pleading with me not to leave her when I dropped her off at my neighbor's home. But my goal was to create a good life for us. If getting one step closer to my goal meant that I had to stand up at seven-thirty in the morning and call people, then I was going to do that. Many times, people would hang up on me during those calls, but I was determined to stay in the game.

At one point I accompanied my cold calling with going house to house, knocking on people's doors. I introduced myself, asking them if they were interested in selling their home. Many times I got a door slammed in my face, but generally people were friendly, listened to my brief introduction, and took my card. As I continued my prospecting, I started sending mail to my prospecting areas. I would send a marketing piece to my new client list about the local market with my name, number, and photo on it. It is crucial to be consistent in your prospecting in the real estate business. Think of ways to meet and speak to new people. You need to put yourself in front of them as often as possible, in a professional way. I've maintained this practice to this day, prospecting regularly and sending approximately fifty thousand postcards a month to a demographic that I feel works for me.

REFLECTIONS: YOU IN CONTACT

▶ I was sometimes cautioned by experienced agents not to waste my time mailing. Just keep in mind that as people throw away your mailer, they will see your name.

▶ When talking to new prospects, have an idea of what you're going to say.

▶ Even if you get a door slammed in your face, remember it's not personal. Keep going and don't give up.

Learning the Inventory of Properties in Your Marketplace

A thorough working knowledge of your marketplace is imperative to your success in real estate. It makes no difference which city or town you live in or whether your particular market is experiencing a real estate boom or a less active market. You must accept current market conditions as you find them. The current condition is not the determining factor in your ability to sell homes; you are. Throughout your real estate career you will experience many different markets and their ups and downs. It is often said that real estate moves in cycles. You can better weather these changes if you understand the basics of the buying and selling trends in your area. This information is critical for you to know in order to advise your prospects and lead them appropriately.

To understand your local market, take the time to study all of the statistics and learn to interpret real estate information about the homes that are for sale or have recently sold in your area. I would suggest reviewing homes that sold within the last three months in a market where properties are selling quickly. In a slower market, there may be flat or depreciative values. In any event, you need to be completely comfortable with the information you are learning so you can explain it intelligently to your prospects, clients, friends, and family. You need to be prepared to answer questions about the real estate market from everyone. Once people know that you're in real estate, they will be excited to ask your opinion. Sometimes I would be at the grocery store, and the butcher or the produce man would ask me what's going on in the real estate market. When I would attend Vanessa's school functions, everyone would be curious about the areas in which they lived. It was important for me to look at everyone as a potential prospect. My preparedness and knowledge of the marketplace and trends made people comfortable. It was clear to people that I cared about my business, that I took it seriously, and that I was thorough and diligent about my job. Each time I left them with the impression that I would work hard and smart for them.

Make sure that you schedule time to preview the real estate market each week. The easiest and most reliable way to stay informed and up to date is through your local multiple listing service (MLS). This invaluable service provides all real estate agents with information regarding available homes for sale, homes that have sold, and expired listings. An expired listing refers to a property that didn't sell within the term of the contract agreed to by the seller and agent, and it may be available to be listed by another agent. The MLS will give you the opportunity to share accurate information with your prospects. Buyers and sellers do rely on you to guide them. Remember you are the leader of your team. You are in charge and will be expected to know how to take them through the process of buying or selling a home.

Encourage your prospects and clients not only to take into consideration the prices of homes that are on the market, but also the prices of homes that have sold. It is important for them also to know the length of time it took properties to sell. Since you have already taken the time to review these statistics, you will be able to point out the importance of pricing a property correctly and how price relates to the time a property takes to sell. We will go into this in more depth later, but the concept is simple. If a property is priced correctly, it sells for a higher price in a shorter period of time. Stop for a moment and think about this idea. Can you understand why this would be the case? If a property is well priced, it will be more desirable to a greater number of buyers. Therefore, there will be a heightened sense of urgency among buyers to make a strong offer. Healthy competition usually begets healthy offers. The longer an unwanted property sits on the market, the less likely a buyer is to step forward with a strong offer. Undoubtedly, your buyers will ask you if the property is priced appropriately. So be prepared!

You can study the marketplace through other venues besides gathering information from the MLS. It would be a good idea to preview firsthand as many open houses as you can in your area. In many communities there are open houses for brokers to preview properties during the week. These broker open houses usually occur once or twice a week, so it gives you several opportunities to see property.

Open houses are usually held by the agent representing the seller of the home. The broker open houses serve a very important purpose, which is to expose the property to the agent community not the public, and they offer a convenient way for agents to see homes and preview them for their potential buyers. It is also a great way to learn the inventory as homes come on the market for sale and to see what activity and interest the house is receiving.

The public open houses are open to everyone and are usually held on Sunday afternoons and sometimes Saturday afternoons as well. Regularly attending these open houses offers you an opportunity to learn even more about the local inventory but also offers a chance to get a feel for floor plans, styles, and the homes that sell quickly in your area. When you have actually seen the inventory of homes and walked through various properties, you will be better able to describe the comparable homes to your clients, If the homes have already sold and you had the chance to preview them when they were on the market, you can give your clients valuable information not otherwise available to them.

REFLECTIONS: LEARNING THE INVENTORY

▶ Make a plan of the first five steps you'll take to learn the inventory of homes for sale in your area.

▶ See as many homes as possible so you can let prospective buyers and sellers know how informed you are about your marketplace.

Building Rapport

What is rapport? It's a relationship, a connection built upon an understanding between you and your prospect. Building rapport with your prospect is essential to the process of buying and selling homes. When you establish rapport with people, it becomes easier to discuss important concerns. You will already have an understanding of their needs, which helps you both speak the same language and develop a level of trust. Once you've reached this level of comfort and confidence, your mind doesn't have to race to understand your client's question or ponder an answer to it.

How do you establish rapport? Ask questions, but be interested and interesting. Go slowly. Don't bombard your prospect with question after question. Listen more than you speak. Be interested in your prospect's responses, and when you do speak, say something interesting. Don't just talk to hear yourself talk. Building rapport is not about selling yourself; it's about making a connection and creating a sense of comfort and confidence between you and your client. After you feel you have built a solid rapport, then begin to ask more detailed questions. If you are talking with a potential seller, you will need to ask questions such as, When would you like to move? What price do you feel your home is worth? Do you need to sell before you buy? In the event you may be speaking with a buyer, some valuable questions to ask might be, Have you been pre-qualified for a loan? What style of home are you looking for? Do you have children and are schools or parks important to you? Some of these conversations will contribute to building rapport with your prospects by addressing their needs. Now you can confidently begin to hold open houses, list and show properties, and make solid connections.

Open Houses

Now that you're on your way and are developing your database of prospects, you will need to begin holding Sunday open houses. A Sunday open house gives you the opportunity to meet the neighbors. They may be interested in selling their home or know coworkers, friends, or family members who might be interested in buying the house that you're holding open. Remember, neighbors love their neighborhood! Although you may not have listings of your own, it would be valuable to hold an open house for an agent in your company, if the opportunity is available to you.

One great example of this was when I had a listing that was on the market for more than four months. In fact, the many agents who had sat the house all those months during open houses told me that they didn't want to sit the house anymore. They told me that they couldn't meet any good buyers that way. So I put a notice out asking if anyone in our company wanted to sit this Sunday open house. The sellers were very anxious and wanted this house sold and were pressuring me to keep this house open every weekend. I received a call from a young woman who told me she was new to the business and wanted to hold it open. I eagerly said yes. The

Sunday open house hours were from two o'clock to five o'clock, and she called me at three and said she had a very interested buyer. After several discussions over the next few hours she did write an offer showing he was a qualified buyer, and in less than twenty-four hours she got an offer accepted and made the sale.

Your goal should be to meet as many people as you possibly can and with luck find several people who are interested in buying and selling with you. It would be helpful for you to place real estate open house signs around the area of the property you're holding open. Try to make sure the signs have your name on them and try to place them where as many people as possible will see them. At your open house, you should have informational sheets about the home and about yourself that your visitors can take with them.

Stand by the front door so that when people come in they have to walk by you. That gives you a chance to introduce yourself. It's also the perfect time for you to get their names and contact information (phone number, e-mail address). Be prepared to write the information down. Agents usually have open house visitors sign themselves in. From experience, I can tell you that you will get more accurate contact information if you write it down yourself. People are more likely to give you their contact information if you look them in the eye, smile, and say, "Hi, I'm Susan from XYZ Real Estate Company. Welcome to my open house. May I have your name and number? Would it be all right if I contacted you?"

Usually, people will be honest with you on the spot, since you've shown interest in them and appreciation that they've come to your open house. Too often I see seasoned agents take open house visitors for granted. They don't bother to introduce themselves, greet them properly, or ask them if they need assistance. They simply tell them where the informational sheets are, tell them to sign in and to let them know if they have any questions. If you were a potential buyer or seller, how would you feel? After your visitors have toured the house and are passing you at the front door to leave, be prepared with questions to ask them. Don't let them leave without engaging in another conversation. Ask them what they thought of the house, if they'd be interested in seeing it a second time, and if they are currently working with an agent. This is your moment to convert a prospective buyer into an active client.

Not long ago, I tried an experiment. Since I don't personally sit Sunday open houses anymore, I decided to visit one with a buyer. I was dressed casually so the other agents didn't recognize me. I went into the open house. I was not asked to sign in. The agents were friendly but told me to go ahead and look around the house. None of the agents there asked me one question! "Hi, welcome" and "Good-bye" were all I heard. After previewing the house I went outside and began talking to other people who were coming out of the open house. I asked them what they thought about the house. I engaged them in a conversation that demonstrated my knowledge of the marketplace. Three of these people asked me if I was an agent and if I would work with them. The lesson is that if you have an open house, just smiling and welcoming people does nothing to sell the home and nothing for you in terms of meeting prospective buyers and sellers. If you hold a Sunday open house, it's for the purpose of selling the home and meeting new people. You must do your professional job and talk to the visitors. So make the effort!

A very different type of story is about a new agent named Joe. Joe was very eager to hold Sunday open houses, and because he had no listings, he asked me every Sunday if I had a house he could hold open. He had an outgoing personality and seemed to be learning the business quickly, so I decided to give him one of my houses to hold open on Sunday. The following Monday morning I asked him how it went. He told me that he didn't get any leads on any serious buyers. He told me that he greeted them and showed them around the home but that he saw most of the prospects as looky-loos, people who were just looking and not real buyers. Joe asked me if he could sit again the following Sunday. He called me afterward and seemed discouraged about not being able to meet any new buyers. I encouraged him to hold the house open once again. Only this Sunday would be different, because I would be with him. I felt Joe had promise, with his upbeat attitude and personality, but perhaps as a new agent he lacked a few communication skills. So I decided we would do this open house together. That Sunday as people came into the open house I engaged them in conversation in front of Joe, asking potential buyers what they thought of the home and what they might be looking for. It was so much fun. In conversation after conversation we were able to establish which people liked this home and to whom we could show other

properties. Together Joe and I created five new qualified prospects in just two hours by asking questions and being interested in our visitors' needs. It was great for me to see Joe gain
so much confidence, and he was well on his way to making a
number of sales. After all, it isn't enough to have an outgoing
or engaging personality if you don't have the right skills and
tools to create a real estate relationship with each person
who walks through the door. When meeting people, you need
to use every opportunity to ask questions so if the house you
are holding open is not right for the buyers, you'll have set up
a relationship and will be able to show them other homes in
the future.

REFLECTIONS: OPEN HOUSE SKILLS

▶ Hold an open house regularly.

▶ Get comfortable talking to people whom
you don't know.

▶ Ask new prospects if they are working with
another agent.

▶ Ask new prospects if they intend to sell their
home before buying.

Many times I have walked away from an open house or a chance meeting with a customer mentally kicking myself for all the things I could have, should have, wished I would have said, but didn't.

I clearly remember my first Sunday open house, but not because of something I said. I got to the house early, turned on all the lights, pulled back the curtains, and staged the house to look its best to potential buyers. I always made sure that I had enough time to get ready and get my bearings before visitors began to arrive. This time I decided to return a few phone calls. At that time, we didn't have cell phones, so I went into the seller's kitchen and used his phone. There wasn't anything too unusual or particularly special about the layout of his kitchen. It had all the standard appliances in all the usual places. It also had a bird, a big bird that could speak. It was a screaming, mimicking parrot. Whenever people came into the house and I tried to have a conversation with them, the parrot would scream at the top of his lungs, as if he were talking. I dreaded that bird. During a lull in the open house I went back into the kitchen to use the phone and finish making calls. Out of the blue that bird started mimicking me and repeating what I was saying. He sounded just like me, only at a higher decibel. He screamed, "Vanessa," "Oh, damn," "Hello, how are you?" He kept getting louder and louder, and then he said, "I hate that bird." I nearly died. I hung up the phone; my heart was racing. I was afraid this bird would repeat these things to the owner when he returned. To say the least, I watched what I said around that bird from then on. It was a good wake-up call, reminding me to be careful what I say and to whom. You never know who or what might be listening.

REFLECTIONS: OPEN HOUSE QUESTIONS

▶ If you found the perfect home, would you buy it right away?

▶ What price range is comfortable for you?

▶ What style home do you prefer?

▶ Does the style of this home work for you?

▶ What areas of the city interest you?

▶ What's important about the areas you prefer?

▶ How soon would you like to buy?

▶ Do you have questions or concerns about the buying process that I can help you with?

▶ Where do you live now?

▶ What do you like or dislike about your current neighborhood?

▶ Are school systems important to you?

▶ Where is your workplace located?

There were Sundays when I really didn't want to face that bird, but I did. I held that house open until it sold. As if from the heavens, one Sunday a buyer walked in during my open house. He wrote an offer and the seller accepted it. That's the thing with Sunday open houses—you have to be prepared to expect the unexpected, and sometimes you'll get a wonderful surprise.

Following Up Leads

So now you've constructed a database, you're doing Sunday open houses, and you're accumulating leads. That's great, but now you have to do something with them. You have to act upon these leads in an intelligent, organized, and professional manner. How do you differentiate between leads? Are they all of equal importance? Do you deal with them in the order in which you received them? Do you work with them in the order of your buyers' and sellers' time frames? What if someone comes through your open house who's really nice and eager to look but doesn't want to buy a home for another year? How about a seller who is up for a job transfer and may have to move out of state within the next two months?

I find it too difficult to follow up with people who are not seriously ready to buy or sell within thirty days from meeting with me. It always leaves me with an uneasy feeling of being in limbo. I commit 110 percent to my clients and customers and I expect the same consideration from them. You may feel differently. However, I can tell you that if you find you're spending large amounts of time convincing people to do something, it's not a good lead. It's like forcing a square peg into a round hole. It's important to your success as a real estate agent to work with people who are serious about making a commitment, are motivated to buy and sell, and who are financially qualified to do so. Trust me, when you work with a lead who is not motivated, the time you spend can adversely affect *your* motivation.

Bottom line, working with people who have no urgency to buy or sell a property not only affects your self-esteem but your ability to earn a living. Enough of these kind of leads can put you in such a funk that your judgment can become clouded. They can cause you to overlook completely the good leads and other clients you may have the chance to represent. So spend the time qualifying your leads and asking questions.

Make sure that you understand your prospects' needs and requirements. Categorize your leads.

CATEGORY	WANT TO BUY/SELL IN
A—Hot	30 days or less
B—Warm	60 days or less
C—Lukewarm	90 days or less

You should call your hot leads daily. Call your warm leads three times a week and lukewarm leads at least once a week. Find the most convenient and comfortable way in which to communicate with your prospects on a regular basis. This can be through mailing updates to your C list to mailing property sheets daily to your A list. Keep in mind that this is the list of potential prospects with whom you have chosen to work and believe will buy and sell with you. The decisions you make regarding whom you spend your time with will ultimately determine your income. Remember, your valuable time is being used for free until you have closed a sale.

REFLECTIONS: FOLLOWING UP

▶ Make a logical plan of how to contact your database. E-mail? Phone? Mailer?

▶ Decide whom to call first.

▶ Identify your good leads. Recognize which leads to pursue.

▶ Set up a system to stay in touch with your leads.

Mastering Your Paperwork

Ask your office to provide you with copies of all the paperwork required for a transaction. Read it all carefully, become familiar with it, and ask questions of your manager or training director if you don't understand what something means.

Contact your local real estate board or check with your office regarding the use of real estate purchase contracts. Be intimately familiar with them and what they mean. As I mentioned before, you will be expected to explain to a buyer or seller every document that they are signing during the course of every transaction.

Real estate contracts can vary from state to state. All of the contract and paperwork procedures may seem complicated at first glance, and you may feel a bit nervous and unsure of how to use them. As you complete more and more transactions, it will become easier, and you'll make fewer mistakes. You will eventually master the contract and closing procedures. It may just take a little bit of time to get used to the process.

REFLECTIONS: BEGINNING PAPERWORK

▶ Be organized.

▶ Keep files.

▶ Keep copies.

Looking the Part

Always think about how you look. Dress professionally when going into the office, on showings, when holding open houses or anytime you are professionally in public. When you feel fully present and properly prepared, you will naturally feel stronger and will approach any situation with confidence.

Remember, this is a business, not a hobby. Take the time to think about how you feel, what you look like, and the message you are conveying. If you were looking at yourself from the perspective of a potential client, would you see yourself as a real estate professional? It doesn't matter where in the world you are working; you'll want to stand apart by presenting a professional appearance. Since you will be smiling a lot, it is important that your dental hygiene is good. Whether it's your hair, hands, car, or clothes, being clean is crucial. Be aware of how you look and how others perceive you. Each time you go out, check to make sure you look your best. Don't go to the store or do errands thinking that you won't run into anyone you know. That's just the time you will! Make sure your clothes are always pressed and cleaned.

One morning when I was in a hurry to get ready, I took a blue suit from my closet. It was my favorite outfit because it gave me a strong professional appearance and the material didn't wrinkle. I could wear it, hang it, and wear it another day. I had important appointments that day and I wanted to look and feel my best. I completed my outfit with a crisp white blouse and headed out the door. I dropped Vanessa off next door at my neighbor's. I felt good. I felt professional. I had my schedule organized, and I was eager to start my work day.

I stopped by the gas station to fill up and have the engine of my Volkswagen checked. It was always overheating, and I was worried that it might happen that day. I couldn't afford for that to derail my schedule. I swung the door of my car open and stepped out. "Excuse me, ma'am," the attendant said. I really didn't like being called ma'am, but I smiled politely and acknowledged him. "You have something on the back of your jacket," he said. I thanked him for discovering it and asked him to brush it off. He swiped at it a few times. I asked if my jacket was okay, but the attendant told me the stain was still there and couldn't be brushed off. I thought this guy was trying to get me to take off my jacket, and all I could think of was that I really didn't want to do that. I was nervous because that morning I had been in a hurry getting dressed, and I had to wear a black bra under my white shirt. So, a bit irritable, I took my jacket off anyway. There it was, cascading down the back of my blue jacket—dry baby throw-up. My best advice to you is it pays to check out your clothes before you leave the house, and don't look at just the front of your outfit.

REFLECTIONS: LOOK PROFESSIONAL

▶ Wear clothes that make you feel professional.

▶ Put together a couple of professional-looking outfits from what you currently own.

▶ For suggestions on dressing for work, go to www.workingwomentoday.com.

Showing Property

When you represent the sellers, you show the property for them. You are hired to sell the home within a specific time frame, preferably in the shortest time possible for the greatest amount of money. You are expected to do this in a professional manner. Always arrive early and prepare the house to be viewed by the buyers and buyers' agent. Turn the lights on, make sure that the beds are made and the animals are secured. Be familiar with the property and be able to answer all questions. When showing the house, make sure your presentation flows properly from the front door on throughout the home.

When representing the buyer, you have a different set of responsibilities. You will be expected to research appropriate properties in the buyers' price range that suit their needs. This search will need to cover their style, size and location preferences, and any other needs. Most likely, you will end up showing a number of houses so that the buyers will have a basis for comparison from which to make a decision. At this point, they will choose the home that they feel best suits their lifestyle and perception of themselves. Don't say too much. Your job is to make the buyers' dreams come true, not pass judgment on their taste in houses. What they may like, you may not like. There is a buyer, whom I will call John, to whom I have sold three houses over the years. It seemed every home I hated, he loved. I had some very embarrassing moments giving my negative opinion on a house that John ultimately would buy. Talk about wanting to eat your words! The lesson I learned was to keep my mouth shut.

Don't worry if you feel nervous or unsure the first few times you get in front of a potential buyer or seller. It's perfectly natural to feel that way. You might be concerned that she will ask you something you don't know. Honestly, there *will* be things you won't know. To this day, after eighteen years in real estate, I still get a question every once in a while that I can't answer. I never guess; I never make up a response if I don't know. I simply and calmly promise to find out the answer and get back to them. This is a much better and more honest approach. It's been my experience that people appreciate honesty. Knowing that I will tell them the truth, they are happy to hear from me and are more likely to put their trust in me to find them a home.

As a new agent, you may not be able to tell when your prospects are being honest with you or giving you truthful feedback. You may get a feeling that your customers are withholding information from you about their particular needs and desires. Some of the reasons could be the result of financial or emotional situations that they feel uncomfortable sharing with you at the moment. However, it is important for you to know if they are working with other agents at the same time that you're showing them property. Otherwise, you may be spinning your wheels and forfeiting the opportunity to work with other buyers who are willing to work with you exclusively. As you begin to recognize the signs of clients working with multiple agents, you will learn to trust your intuition.

REFLECTIONS: SHOWING

▶ When representing the seller, be early and prepare the house for the showing.

▶ When representing the seller, make a plan of how you will show the house.

▶ When representing the buyer, will you show the most inexpensive or expensive homes first?

▶ When representing the buyer, will you show homes that need work or that don't need work first?

Making Progress

As you build and grow your business, be sure to make a weekly appointment with your manager to monitor your progress. Even if you are consistently working every day to build your real estate business, you could easily get off track or lose your focus. There will be a lot of new information being given to you and a lot to learn each day. Having a manager to help you stay on track and sort through and explain things is invaluable.

There is always more to learn, and that should be looked upon as an exciting facet of this business. You may not be able to grasp every concept the first time around, but know that if you make a mistake and misunderstand a concept, you can and will recover. Often, those experiences are part of a natural learning process.

As the saying goes, "You can't win them all." This is definitely true about real estate. You won't list every house in your area; you won't sell every buyer in your marketplace. But with nearly 300 million homes of all kinds in the United States, there is plenty of business for everyone. I currently work in a marketplace where there are approximately eleven thousand licensed real estate agents. Yet there are still plenty of buyers and sellers who need representation. So don't allow setbacks to throw you off course. Just because things don't work out as planned and you don't get the opportunity to represent a particular buyer or seller, don't lose sight of your goal and other opportunities. You absolutely cannot have success without failure. So buck up!

Things I Need to Finish

The most successful people you will find in life never put off anything that can be done today. They know what needs to be done and do it.

Throughout the day, keep a running list of things that need to be accomplished. I call this page "Things I Need to Finish." At the end of the day, put on a new list those things that you feel you can finish the next day. This list will help prioritize the most important things that need your attention first. By following this list, you will find you've accomplished a little each day. If you truly want to be successful, you'll need to complete daily activities and know that they will lead you straight to your goals. If you find that you have no time left in your day, fill out a weekly calendar and write what you need to do each day, hour by hour. It will help you take inventory to evaluate where you might have more available time or how you can be more effective in areas that you may not have considered before.

Eye on the Competition

Real estate is a very competitive profession. As you're learning, it takes a lot of focus, consistency, determination, and sheer will to become successful. As real estate professionals, we have to learn to navigate through a multitude of interpersonal relationships and egos. At times, we have to play psychiatrist, lawyer, friend, and parent to our clients. These client relationships will come and go through your career, and they often change over the course of a transaction. However, the relationships that last will be those that you forge with your fellow agents, the people with whom you work day in and day out. The relationships we have with our colleagues in such a competitive environment are not like any others in the business world. You will most likely be closer to the agents in your office than in other companies because you have a stronger bond. However, the fact remains that we are independent contractors and by definition are one another's competition. We all compete for sales in the same marketplace.

REFLECTIONS: BEING EFFICIENT

▶ Have a good understanding of where you spend most of your time.

▶ Classify your daily activities, from most important to least important.

▶ At the end of the day, recount which activities you have accomplished, from the most to the least important.

▶ Review whether you could have been more productive.

Whoever, wherever the competition is, we walk a very fine line of trust and integrity with one another. The truth is we really need to cooperate to be successful. Although in many situations you may be competitors, once the deal is accepted by all parties, you are partners. You need to be supportive and work toward the same goal—the successful close of the sale.

You will undoubtedly encounter unethical behavior from time to time in this industry. Keep your composure, stay your course, and represent your client with integrity. If a deal falls apart because you had little or no cooperation from the other agent, move on and sell your client another home. Do not allow the emotions of any situation to affect your relationship with your client or alter your advice to him. In the end, what will shine through will be your willingness to deal confidently and calmly in a highly charged emotional situation, without losing your sense of purpose or compromising your duty to protect and watch over your client's needs.

There may be times when you will be unsure of what to say in conversations with your prospective clients. The following chapter will give you some basic ideas of how conversations may go when calling contacts in your database, holding an open house, or showing and listing property.

REFLECTIONS: BE AWARE

▶ Read publications that can give you new ideas and send pertinent articles to your clients.

▶ Notice how your competitors are advertising.

▶ Find out why someone is getting more business than you.

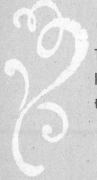

Take the first step in faith. You don't have to see the whole staircase, just take the first step.

—MARTIN LUTHER KING, JR.

CHAPTER SIX

Doing It!

In any situation when speaking with a potential client, you need to pause and reflect on what you're going to say and how you're going to respond. Remember when having these conversations as a real estate professional, this is not the time to share your personal information with her as you would with your best friend. Since none of us are perfect, we've all said things at the wrong time or responded inappropriately, especially when we're under stress. You're not alone. Acknowledge the mistake in the situation and move on.

As the professional leading your buyers and sellers into making one of the most important decisions of their lives, you need to control your emotions. It is human nature that the people with whom you'll be dealing will be emotional. Stay cool, don't be bullied, take a professional stand, count to ten if you need to, and never let them know that you need the deal. Once you compromise your integrity, you become the doormat. I remember a very specific time in my career when a seller was completely freaking out during the process of selling his home and out of the blue he spit on me. I actually just paused, looked at him, and walked away. I didn't take his calls over the next few days. My detachment forced him to come around, get control of himself and his emotions, and apologize to me.

Database Dialogue

Now that you have your database set up, you've created the foundation you will use to build your business. Once it begins working for you, it will be a great networking tool and referral source. When you begin to call contacts in your database, remember to first call the people you know the best and with whom you feel most comfortable. Don't forget to speak with confidence and enthusiasm when discussing your new profession in real estate. You will be more focused if you are calling from your designated work space, and remember the trick of standing up in front of your desk, as I did. This will be more than a casual conversation; think of this as a business call. Whether you're calling a friend, family member, neighbor, or former coworker, be professional, positive, and informative. In this chapter, I'll give you some samples of different calls you might make when working your contact database.

CALL TO A FORMER COWORKER

MIKE: Hello, windows and door department, this is Mike, may I help you?

GINA: The question is, may I help you? Hi Mike, it's Gina.

MIKE: Gina, hey, we were just talking about you yesterday. We all got your announcement that you're in real estate now. Nice business card. How's it going?

COMMENTARY: *A few months is too long to wait to call your database contacts. It would be a good idea to start calling as soon as you are set up for business. Remember, this is the beginning of building your business.*

GINA: It's going great. I'm really happy. My parents' friends, the Mosers, listed their house with me and I sold it.

MIKE: I'll bet that means that you don't miss us.

GINA: Of course I do! I'll always miss you guys. Only now I'm available to help you and your friends buy or sell your homes.

MIKE: That's what we were talking about on our break yesterday. Joan said that she looked at a house over the weekend, and Mary asked if you showed it to her.

GINA: No, I didn't show her a home. She didn't call me.

MIKE: She mentioned that she had forgotten that you were in real estate now. Then she remembered that she had received your card and said she must have misplaced it between the bills and the kids' homework. Mary did give her your number again, but you should send her another card and call her yourself.

GINA: Thanks for telling me. I'll send her another card and call her right away. She's still at extension #2556, isn't she?

MIKE: Yes, she'll be happy to hear from you. Don't be a stranger now that you're a super Realtor!

GINA: Don't be silly, Mike, we'll always be friends. I would be thrilled to help all of you.

COMMENTARY: *Make sure that Mike knows that you are sincere. Even though you are interested in procuring business, your sentiments should come from the heart.*

MIKE: Well, Gina, I have a customer, so I have to go, but do give Joan a call.

COMMENTARY: *This is a good learning experience about the value of a database. It's important to call your contacts immediately and on a regular basis. Keep in touch with them often. Even if you're busy and already have a few sellers and buyers, developing your business is an ongoing process and you must keep at it constantly. Have you ever heard of the expression, "Out of sight, out of mind"? Your clients will forget about you* *if you aren't communicating with them regularly. Don't let that happen to you.*

JOAN: Hello, this is Joan.

GINA: Hi Joan, this is Gina.

JOAN: Gina, I'm so glad you called. I misplaced your card, and we're thinking of selling our house and buying a new one.

GINA: I'd love to help you; it would be so much fun.

JOAN: And we have so much to catch up on!

COMMENTARY: *You are no longer coworkers, you are agent and client. Don't blur the professional boundaries. Sometimes sharing too much personal information with clients can be inappropriate, even with clients you've known for a long time. Keep in mind that buying and selling a home can be stressful for the buyers and sellers. This is the wrong time to discuss any of your own personal information.*

GINA: I can't believe that you're moving. I know how much you love your house and neighborhood. What prompted you to consider buying a new house?

COMMENTARY: *It's important to establish the client's motivation for moving. It will clarify her reason for buying and selling and give you an idea of her time frame. Remember the thirty-, sixty-, and ninety-day rule!*

JOAN: Well, with the kids getting older and Donna starting college next year, we thought that we might scale down to a smaller home. We would like to stay in the neighborhood.

GINA: I can't believe that Donna is all grown up and ready for college. How are the twins doing?

JOAN: They're fourteen and active as ever. They really love their school and spending time with their friends. That's why I want to stay in the area. I really don't want to disrupt their lives too much.

GINA: Those are valid considerations, Joan. Plus your neighborhood is so convenient to everything. How many bedrooms do you currently have? Four, if I remember correctly?

JOAN: Yes, but we really use one of them as a den. We have a sleeper sofa in there just in case my in-laws come to visit.

GINA: When you think of scaling down, what do you have in mind? What are some of the things that you'd be willing to give up? Fewer bedrooms?

JOAN: Three bedrooms would be fine. We still do need a yard, because now we have a puppy.

GINA: That will keep you busy! As a matter of fact, I have recently seen a few smaller three-bedroom homes with yards in your neighborhood. Have you discussed with your husband a price range that would be comfortable?

COMMENTARY: *This is a great example of how valuable it is to visit broker and public open houses and to see the inventory. By personally seeing homes, you will be able to discuss them with your clients in detail. The more knowledgeable you are about properties in your area, the more secure your clients will feel about working with you.*

JOAN: Yes my husband and I have discussed price ranges. What we can afford to pay for our next house would depend on how much we can get for this house. From what I've seen from Sunday open houses, our house is probably worth about $350,000.

GINA: Sometimes it's hard to figure out values looking at the listed prices. I'd be happy to come over and talk to you in person about these things. That way, I could see your home again and give you an estimate of its value. I'll bring with me information about which homes have sold in your area and for how much, and that will give you a better idea of what to expect. I'll also bring some information on the three-bedroom houses that are listed for sale. If you like any of them, I'll set up appointments so we can see the ones that are interesting to you.

JOAN: Fantastic! I'm so glad you called.

GINA: Me too. When would you like me to come to the house?

JOAN: Tonight around seven thirty would be great. My husband will be home by then. It will be wonderful to see you.

GINA: I'll see you then.

COMMENTARY: *Even though you have an appointment tonight with Joan and her husband, immediately move on to calling the next person in your database. Keep calling people whether you've had a successful call or not. Schedule your calls for the same time every day and stick to it. Be positive and expect that business will naturally develop from this important exercise. Once you have a system of calling, you can choose to call your database contacts alphabetically. Or perhaps you'll call family, friends, acquaintances, or former coworkers first, or you may choose to call people who live in the various areas where you prefer to work. It's like taking baby steps. You need to walk before you can run. Stay the course and be methodical and systematic.*

CALL TO A FAMILY MEMBER

KATHY: Hello, this is Kathy.

GINA: It's your cousin Gina. How are you?

KATHY: Fine, fine. I got your real estate announcement. What great news! Congratulations! I heard that the Mosers asked you to help them sell their house.

GINA: They did. I listed it and sold it quickly.

KATHY: Wow! You must love what you're doing.

GINA: Yes, I really like real estate. It felt so good to be able to help the Mosers. Remember when we were kids and Mrs. Moser used to give us Hershey's Kisses when we would visit them? Well, she still had a big bowl of them sitting on that same round table in their entryway. Some things never change.

KATHY: That's funny, I hadn't thought about that in a long time. Did she insist you have some?

GINA: Of course. She offered and I took one for old time's sake. But when I was there, I was focused on getting them the best price for their home and doing a good job. It was really different looking at the house as a professional real estate agent.

COMMENTARY: *It's important that friends and especially family members see you as a professional real estate agent, because they may have a different image of you. Direct them to the person you are today.*

Open House

You are standing at the front door, relaxed, appropriately dressed, and ready to meet and greet people. A prospective buyer comes up the front walkway. An exchange with this prospect might go something like this:

GINA: Welcome, my name is Gina Simmons. I'm the agent holding this open house today.

COMMENTARY: *Look the prospect in the eye, smile, extend your hand, and offer a firm handshake.*

STEVE: I'm Steve Houseman.

GINA: Thank you for coming, Steve. The seller has requested that all guests sign the open house registration form. Would you be willing to leave your contact information as well?

STEVE: I'd be happy to as long as you promise not to bug me.

COMMENTARY: *If he's willing to give you his contact information, chances are it will be okay to call him if you have something to tell him. This would be a good time to smile to establish a rapport with the potential buyer. This is also the time to say, "I will of course only contact you with information that you may find valuable."*

GINA: This is really a great house. May I show you around? This house has some features you may not notice that I'd like to point out to you.

COMMENTARY: *Have a plan for the way you'll show the house. Walk through the house in a way that best shows off the attributes of the floor plan. This will show how easy the rooms will be to live in and how they work for entertaining friends.*

GINA: As you can see, this home has a very open floor plan. Do you like the feel of the rooms?

STEVE: Yeah, I suppose I do. But I've always seen myself in more traditional homes, like the family house I grew up in.

COMMENTARY: *The prospect just made an important comment. Pay attention. He just told you that his vision of the home he is looking for is based on the home he grew up in. You'll hear this comment frequently from buyers. Many times, they'll refer to their childhood home as their frame of reference when envisioning a style. Since you've just met the prospect, you shouldn't ask too many in-depth questions about his childhood. Remember to maintain some personal boundaries, and to make mental notes of comments you may hear.*

GINA: Actually, there was a couple who just left who said they also grew up in a traditional-style home. They really seemed to like the open kitchen/family room combination that this home has. You have to admit, it does work well when making dinner and watching the kids at the same time. Do you have children?

STEVE: Not yet. Is this house only for a family?

COMMENTARY: *This is your opportunity to get clarification of the buyer's needs.*

GINA: Actually, this home can work for many different lifestyles.

STEVE: Well, do you think it would be too big for one, maybe two people?

GINA: Not at all. This home would be great for entertaining. Besides, you would have room to grow in case two turns into three one day.

COMMENTARY: *You can sense that the conversation is flowing easily.*

STEVE: So, how many bedrooms are there?

GINA: The way the house lays out now, it has four bedrooms and three baths.

STEVE: Oh, that sounds big to me, maybe too many bedrooms for my needs.

GINA: Not really, when you consider that one of the bedrooms could easily be used as a home office. Would you need a home office?

STEVE: Maybe. Is it wired with high-speed Internet?

GINA: Yes. This room does have high-speed computer lines, a built-in work area, and many other features.

COMMENTARY: *Now you've piqued his interest. Take him to see the room right away so he can experience feeling it as "his" home office.*

GINA: Do you work from home now?

STEVE: Only on weekends.

GINA: And what do you do?

STEVE: I'm an attorney.

COMMENTARY: *Well, it certainly seems like you may have an interested buyer here because you have continuously been discussing the points of the house with him.*

GINA: Aren't you glad that you came to this open house today? You seem to be considering things you may not have thought of before.

COMMENTARY: *You have now given the buyer a good mental image of himself in the house to remember.*

GINA: Look at the great view from the office overlooking the yard. Doesn't it make it pleasant to work from here?

STEVE: Well, the yard is peaceful and very inviting, and it's a great place to entertain. I can see throwing a few parties there.

GINA: Accessing the yard through the French doors in the kitchen makes it a natural for outdoor dining with friends. Do you entertain a lot now?

STEVE: Actually, I do. My friends would *love it* here.

GINA: Do you have a lot of friends in this area? Are you originally from here?

STEVE: No, I'm originally from Chicago.

GINA: How long have you been here?

STEVE: About five years.

GINA: Have you been looking for a home for a long time?

STEVE: I've been thinking about buying a home for a while. I haven't been looking that long, but I'm ready to buy when I find the right home. I really like living here. For the past few years I've been saving up for a down payment on a home. So I guess you could say that I'm fairly ready to buy.

COMMENTARY: *The fact that he's been saving for a down payment means that he's a serious buyer.*

GINA: It's a small world. I met a woman in the park the other day who's in a similar situation. She also moved here from Chicago. Have you ever been to the neighborhood park near here?

COMMENTARY: *He may be thinking of the five years he has already spent here without buying a home. Has he made that commitment in his mind yet?*

STEVE: Is the park that really big one a couple of blocks away from here?

GINA: Yes, I take my dog every morning there to play. There's an area reserved where they can play off leash. Do you have a dog?

COMMENTARY: *Animals are a hot button. Generally, people fall into two categories, either they have them or want them, or they can't understand other people's obsession with them. If you're lucky and your prospect falls into the first category, it's an easy way to form a bond over a common interest. By establishing a bond about his interests you can lead him toward a discussion of the things he likes doing and where he could find them. The topic could be anything—sports, dogs, schools, professions, or children.*

STEVE: No, but I'd like to get one. I would feel bad leaving a dog at home alone all day.

GINA: Well, if you lived here you could work from your home office.

COMMENTARY: *Be pleasant and smile; you know he's interested. This is not the time to be pushy.*

GINA: Seriously, if you had a dog, you could take your puppy to the park regularly. My dog has such a great time at the park and is so exhausted that I don't feel guilty going to work and leaving him at home. Do you ever go to a gym?

COMMENTARY: *Mentioning the gym is another avenue to find out what the buyer's needs are as well as learning more about his hobbies and interests.*

STEVE: Is there a gym nearby? I try to go at least three days a week. It would be great if one were close by. The one I go to now is a little out of my way.

GINA: There are several I can refer you to. Also, you could easily turn one of the extra bedrooms into a home gym if you wanted.

COMMENTARY: *Realize that now you have him visualizing the home office, the gym, entertaining, and having a dog.*

GINA: It seems like there are many things about this house that would fit your needs. How do you feel about the style, location, and price of this property?

STEVE: I'm surprised, but I like this modern open style. I would never have thought so. Whenever I viewed houses on the Web, I skipped all the ones that said "modern."

GINA: That's why it's important to visit properties in person. The Web serves as an introduction to homes and gives you an overview of the neighborhoods and area prices. However, nothing can replace seeing a house in person. What made you stop by here today?

STEVE: You're right. That's why this morning I decided to go out and look at some homes, and I'm glad that I did.

COMMENTARY: *So he wasn't necessarily looking at this neighborhood, but you can tell you have piqued his interest.*

GINA: If you're unsure about this home, I would be happy to set up appointments to show you other homes. Would that be something you would like to do?

STEVE: I would like to see more homes. I do appreciate that you've been listening to my needs and concerns.

GINA: As an agent, I always listen and take note of what's important to my clients. Please, be sure to tell me what you like and don't like. Be perfectly candid with me so that I don't have to guess what you want or make assumptions. For example, I might assume that this is a good location for you since you came to this open house.

STEVE: Yes, this is a very convenient location, but I would like to look in other areas as well.

GINA: Is this a comfortable price range for you?

STEVE: Yes it is. At some point I would like to figure out what my monthly payments would be.

GINA: That would depend on the loan program you choose along with your down payment. I could refer you to a loan broker if you don't have one already. That way you will have a better understanding about your payments and your price range. It will also be important for both of us to know your financial options before proceeding further in your home search.

STEVE: I understand. I wouldn't want to fall in love with a house that I couldn't really afford. And you wouldn't want to do a lot of work for nothing.

COMMENTARY: *The prospect seems to be inquiring if you will assist him with the prequalification process and help him find a lender. This is an educational time for the prospect. He will receive information regarding his monthly payments and financial obligations and will rely upon you to help him understand it. This is also a learning experience for you. You will learn that this is a step toward a sale, not a guarantee that one will be consummated.*

GINA: I would like to assist you in finding a home that you're comfortable purchasing. Being prequalified gives you a better understanding of your financial capabilities so that when you do fall in love with a house you can buy it.

COMMENTARY: *By offering to assist the buyer with suggestions that he get prequalified, you make it clear to the client that this is business. If the client's intention to purchase a home is serious, this will be valuable information to him. If he isn't serious, then he'll have excuses not to speak to a lender.*

STEVE: That's great to know.

GINA: I will be happy to give you the name of a mortgage broker I work with a lot. Once you've spoken with him and you're comfortable with the direction you want to go, let me know.

COMMENTARY: *Give another gentle reminder to your prospect that it is important to get preapproved for a loan. Let him know that once you make an offer on his behalf for a property, his offer will be stronger if accompanied with a letter of preapproval from a reputable lender.*

GINA: I really appreciate your openness and the opportunity to be part of the process of finding a home for you. This is my card. Thank you for your information. Of course it will remain confidential. I'll call you on Tuesday to check in with you. If you need referrals to mortgage brokers, let me know, and I'd be happy to assist you with any references you may need.

COMMENTARY: *As you get to know people, they will feel a sense of safety when working with you. That will give them the confidence that you'll listen to their needs and help them understand the process of buying a home. Make sure that they know that what they tell you about themselves is confidential.*

STEVE: Thank you. I appreciate your time and help.

COMMENTARY: *Smile, always look the prospect in the eye, and give him a firm handshake.*

GINA: It was great meeting you, and I really look forward to the opportunity to work with you. Enjoy the rest of your afternoon.

COMMENTARY: *As your prospect is leaving the open house, a large group of people arrive.*

STEVE: It looks like I brought you some good luck. A lot of people are arriving. I'll talk to you during the week.

COMMENTARY: *As this prospect leaves, greet your new visitors. Try to shake hands with everyone, although it may be difficult. If a lot of people show up at the same time to your open house, don't get overwhelmed. Stay at the front door greeting people and shaking hands. Write down their names and numbers while giving them a highlighted overview of the home. This may, after all, be your lucky day!*

GINA: Welcome everyone. Are you looking at this home together?

COMMENTARY: *It's a logistical dilemma when you have groups come in at the same time, because they will all go in different directions. You will need to put your multitasking skills to work!*

GINA: If you'd like, I could show you through the house so you can get a feel for the flow. Or you can also walk through the house yourself.

COMMENTARY: *Close and lock the front door so you can control the flow of people. Do not leave the front door open unsupervised. When you show a home to many people at the same time, none of whom you know, show the house the most straightforward way possible. The flow should make sense and capture the attention of the greatest number of prospects. Try to get them to follow your lead. Since there are too many people for you to ask them all questions, it's best not to focus on specific features of the home. Typically, you would start at the front entry and move through the public rooms first: living room, dining room, family room, and kitchen. If the house has a usable finished basement, show it, too. Then show the bedrooms, saving the master bedroom for last. Proceed to the backyard and all the features of the outdoor spaces. When finishing the tour, take the prospects back through the public rooms to the living room and ask them if they have any questions. If one person in a group asks a number of detailed questions, ask for their contact information so you can speak to them directly later. In time, you'll be able to tell the difference between questions sparked by an interest in the home and those asked just for the sake of asking. It goes back to the material on setting boundaries in chapter 3. Remember, people would call me just because they had my number and they could reach me to ask random questions. Many times, people will walk through Sunday open houses just because they're curious. They may not ever intend to buy a home; they just enjoy looking every Sunday as a source of entertainment. Be careful not to waste your time. Remember, you only have a finite number of hours and an infinite number of tasks to accomplish in your career. Your tasks to accomplish at your Sunday open house are to sell the home for the seller and meet new prospects to grow your business.*

Showing Your Buyer

Steve is now preapproved for a loan and ready to look at houses. He still likes the house you held open on Sunday but would like to see more comparable homes. Also, the house you held open is a stretch financially, which is a concern for him.

You agree to show him other properties, perhaps in a more comfortable price range. While scheduling and showing these homes, make sure that you create a folder with informational sheets on all the houses you're planning to see together in the order in which you'll visit them. Make a packet for him of these appointments and call it a Buyer's Packet. You'll hand this to him before you begin your tour together. You may also want to include a pad of paper and pen for Steve to take notes. If you are showing multiple properties and have the time, it would be a good idea to map them out in a logical route. You want to drive from property to property in the most direct fashion. You need to be organized. If it's your first time out together, I would suggest that you show no more than six homes. You will need to get a feel for how Steve reacts to different homes before showing him more.

As Steve and you visit various homes, pay attention to the feedback he gives you after viewing each property. When another agent is showing you and Steve a home, pay attention to Steve's nonverbal responses. See what makes him smile, and what makes him wrinkle his forehead. Once you are back in the car, if he doesn't volunteer the information, ask him what he was feeling about the home he just toured.

If possible, it would be a good idea for you and Steve to ride together in your car. This way you have the opportunity to discuss the houses that you've visited. You must make sure that your car is clean and not cluttered with miscellaneous papers or garbage, and be sure to have enough gas! Once you arrive to meet the listing agent, introduce yourself and your client and hand the agent your card with your buyer's name on it.

Now that you have converted your open house prospect into a potential buyer and you're out looking at homes together, the conversation during your showings may go something like this:

GINA: Hi, I'm Gina Simmons, and this is my client, Steve Houseman.

LISTING AGENT: I'm David Bader, the listing agent. Thank you for coming. This is a three-bedroom home plus a den. And there are two and a half baths. Would you like me to show you, or would you like to look around yourself? If you have any questions, let me know.

COMMENTARY: *If you haven't seen the house before and don't know the floor plan, ask the agent to give you the tour.*

GINA: Actually, David, since this is a brand-new listing and I haven't had a chance to preview it for Steve, would you mind taking us through the home?

LISTING AGENT: Not at all.

COMMENTARY: *After the listing agent has shown you the home, ask if Steve wants to walk through the home again with you. If he does, ask him questions about how he feels about that particular house.*

GINA: Steve, is this a layout and style that could work for you?

STEVE: It's funny—there are some similarities to the home I grew up in. It's almost like déjà vu.

COMMENTARY: *People's facial expressions rarely lie. Look at Steve's face. Quite possibly—in spite of Steve's wanting a replica of his childhood home—this house won't work for him after all. Often people will end up purchasing a home very different from the one they grew up in.*

GINA: This is only one of the homes we're seeing today. We have five more to go! Let's see them all and then discuss what appeals to you. The next one has a view.

STEVE: Someone at my office was talking about one that just came on the market about a week ago. She said that it had an incredible view of the mountains.

GINA: This may be the home she was talking about. Is a view important to you?

STEVE: It would be nice, but it's not that important. If I had to choose between a view and a yard, I'd rather have a great yard.

COMMENTARY: *That's important information that you've now heard several times. If you recall, Steve really liked the yard at your Sunday open house.*

Now you get into the car and drive to the next house on your list to show Steve. It's a very different home from the ones you've already seen. As you approach the door, the listing agent greets you. Introduce yourself and your buyer. Hand the agent your card with Steve's name on it. You can see that Steve seems to have an almost immediate positive reaction to this home.

STEVE: May I sit in this chair?

LISTING AGENT: By all means.

COMMENTARY: *A seasoned agent will recognize an interested buyer when showing a property and will stop* *talking. This will give the buyer some space to absorb the environment. Again, sit down with your buyer. Your mind might be racing, thinking that the room is dark when you know he likes light and bright. Should you point it out at that moment? No. Say nothing. Let the buyer decide how it feels to him. Remember the person I represented who has very different tastes than I do?*

GINA: How does it feel to you in this space? It's very different from the last house.

COMMENTARY: *Make a mental note that the buyer's response to this home seems different from the previous homes you've seen. He really seems to like this one, although it's very different from what he said he wanted.*

STEVE: It feels strange. I kind of like the look, and yet there's something I don't like about it. What do you think?

COMMENTARY: *Your client is asking for your opinion. This is a subjective question, and you may not have the same point of view. Just remember, you are not the buyer. There will be questions that you cannot answer for the buyer. How he feels or sees his life in a particular home is for him to determine. It's your job to be prepared to know the values of the properties you've seen. While it is great to be the second pair of eyes and ears for your buyer, the truth is we're hired for our professional opinion of value when the buyer finds a home he would like to purchase. What makes one home more valuable than another to a buyer? The answer will be determined by a combination of your professional expertise in assessing the buyer's emotional tie to the house along with his view of its cost. The client needs to know that you feel the house is a good purchase. When he's asking you the question, he's asking if you feel it's okay for him to buy this home.*

GINA: Well, personally, I love the look and appreciate the style. The more important question is whether you like it or not. You seem to respond to openness and light. And this home does have a very sophisticated, warm, and welcoming feeling. I'm showing you a number of homes today with different styles. Let's see them all and then discuss how you feel.

STEVE: I'm looking forward to seeing them all. So far you've chosen interesting properties for me to see.

COMMENTARY: *Once you've spent a reasonable amount of time at a house, or if you begin to hear any frustration, start to move the showing along so you can finish and get to your next appointment.*

GINA: I'm glad there are things you like about this home. Shall we move on and see the other homes?

COMMENTARY: *Keep the conversation positive. Try to remember the things he likes and dislikes in the homes you show so you can discuss them when you're finished.*

Listing Appointment

Once you have an appointment to pitch a potential listing, make sure you drive past the house to see its curb appeal. Look for something outstanding about the exterior, then find a way to discuss it when you meet with the seller. For your appointment, prepare a marketing plan explaining what you will do to get the property sold and include statistics on comparable properties that have sold in the area. You may even want to bring statistics on what homes are listed for sale to show the seller the competition. Look up a history through the public records on the property prior to your appointment. That way, you are aware of all of the home's information.

When you arrive at your appointment and the seller answers the door, look your potential client in the eye, smile, extend your hand, and offer a firm handshake. The conversation may go something like this:

GINA: Hi, I'm Gina Simmons.

MR. TELLER: I'm Arnold Teller. My wife, Edith, is stuck in traffic. She asked me to begin the meeting without her. She didn't want to keep you waiting.

GINA: Thank you for inviting me to come and see your home. Over the years, I've always admired your beautiful roses. Walking up your driveway feels so cheerful and bright.

MR. TELLER: We're very proud of our roses; we both love gardening.

GINA: I remember hearing people comment on them when they came into my Sunday open house down the street.

MR. TELLER: We received your mailer saying that you sold that home. I didn't feel comfortable asking the Mosers, but can you tell me how much it sold for?

COMMENTARY: *Your mailer got them to call you! It may even have made them consider selling, too.*

GINA: It's no problem for me to tell you what it sold for; it's public knowledge. The information for sold properties is easy for people to find in the MLS. The Mosers' house sold for $375,000. I have information with me regarding other properties for sale in your area. First, if you wouldn't mind, I'd love to see your home. That way I'll have a better feel for its value when we talk.

COMMENTARY: *When touring the house, the seller may point out sentimental things to you. Take note. These will be valuable to mention to his wife when you meet her.*

MR. TELLER: Prices have certainly gone up since we bought this home.

GINA: I bet you've seen quite a few changes in the neighborhood since you've been here.

MR. TELLER: Oh yes, my goodness, too many to remember. This was my son's room when he was a little boy.

GINA: He must have been quite an athlete. Look at all those trophies.

COMMENTARY: *Clearly the seller is close to his son and is very nostalgic, since many of his son's accomplishments are still in this room. This is a good clue as to the seller's mind-set. He will probably have an emotional attachment to his home and will expect that from the prospective buyer. If two offers are equal and one is made by a young father with a son, the seller would be more likely to choose that offer.*

MR. TELLER: Yes, he was. He was an all-star Little Leaguer. His mother and I never missed one of his games.

GINA: Does he live in the area now?

MR. TELLER: My son and my daughter-in-law and three grandkids live about an hour away. They would like us to move there.

GINA: Is that why you and Mrs. Teller are considering selling your home? You know, if you need assistance in moving to a new location, I'd be happy to refer an agent in that area.

MR. TELLER: That's very kind of you. Selling our home is a very big step. To do that, we can use all the help we can get.

GINA: It is a life-changing step, but I'm sure it will be wonderful for you to be closer to your son and grandchildren. How long have you lived in this neighborhood?

MR. TELLER: We've lived in the neighborhood for forty-eight years, forty-five years in the house. It was custom built for us back then. I'll let my wife tell you about it.

COMMENTARY: *This is a sign that the wife is probably the one who will make the final decision to move or not. Be aware that Mr. Teller may not be the total decision maker, but his input may still be what brings the deal together at the end.*

GINA: You sound just like my parents. They recently moved to be closer to my brother and his kids. They couldn't be happier.

MR. TELLER: We hope so. We're not spring chickens anymore, and the thought of moving and having people come through our home to see it seems overwhelming.

GINA: Don't worry. It will be fine. Although selling your home can be somewhat disruptive to your life, if you choose to work with me, I will accompany all showings so that strangers won't be left alone in your house. I promise to make it as comfortable as possible. We will be a team all the way through the process.

COMMENTARY: *Edith Teller arrives.*

GINA: Hello, Mrs. Teller, I'm Gina Simmons. Mr. Teller just gave me a tour of your very lovely home.

MRS. TELLER: I'm sure that Arnold told you that we're thinking of moving closer to our son and his family.

GINA: Yes, it sounds very exciting, and I'm happy for you.

MRS. TELLER: Did you discuss price yet?

COMMENTARY: *It appears that Mrs. Teller is the negotiator, and all financial matters should be more directed to her. After all, her first question to you was regarding price.*

MR. TELLER: Not yet, but the Mosers got $375,000 for their house.

MRS. TELLER: Well, ours is twice as nice as their house.

COMMENTARY: *Don't agree or disagree. Just take note of her tone and implied expectation. She wants and expects a better price than $375,000, unlike Mr. Teller, who probably would be happy with $375,000. Remember, he was surprised prices were so high in the area.*

You obviously have two very different personalities and sets of expectations to address. It appears Mr. Teller will care about who buys the house. If it's a family with a young son in Little League, he'll want to sell to them. It seems Mrs. Teller will want someone who sees the value in the house.

GINA: Mrs. Teller, your husband told me that this house was custom built for you. It would be great if you could make a list of all of the features I could share with potential buyers.

MRS. TELLER: Whoever buys this house will love the location and living here and will get their money's worth. This was a very expensive house to build at the time.

COMMENTARY: *Mrs. Teller needs to know that you see the value in her house. Affirm what she believes. She is obviously proud to live there and would like the next buyer to appreciate it too.*

GINA: I'm sure that's true. I'll find a buyer who can really appreciate the house the way you and Mr. Teller have for so many wonderful years. What is your favorite feature of your home?

MRS. TELLER: The central vacuum system. I always believed in keeping a tidy house.

GINA: It shows that you take pride in your home, and as your agent I'll take pride in listing your home if given the opportunity.

MRS. TELLER: So do you think we can get $400,000 for it?

COMMENTARY: *Remember why you're there. Be pleasant and not condescending. Above all, be firm in what you* *believe. Be a leader. You are there to tell the truth and help them get their home sold.*

GINA: I have included some information for you and Mr. Teller about the pricing of your home, as well as my marketing plan. Let's discuss it and go over everything step by step. That way it will all make sense to you. Together, I'm sure we can come up with the proper price for your home, should you make the commitment to sell it.

MRS. TELLER: I already have a price in mind.

COMMENTARY: *Mrs. Teller is clearly anxious. Mr. Teller's silence signals that only Mrs. Teller will make the decision. Even so, be sure to include Mr. Teller in the discussion. Keep it light but firm.*

GINA: That's great, Mrs. Teller. However, let's go over the information together and then talk about the price. How does that sound to both of you?

MRS. TELLER: Fine, let's see what you've brought with you.

COMMENTARY: *Open your listing booklet and have a flyer with a picture of their home on it. This will show an effort on your part to sell their home.*

MR. TELLER: Well, I'll be. Where did you find this?

GINA: I made it especially for you. I drove by yesterday and took the photo. Of course now I'll have real information to put on it since I've seen the house. Once we decide on a price, that would be included as well.

MR. TELLER: Will you send out a mailer like you did for the Mosers' home?

GINA: I'll not only send out mailers to the neighborhood, but when you see the marketing I have planned for your lovely home, I think you'll be very pleased. Your son will even be able to show his children his old bedroom from his computer. I do a lot of online marketing and other things that we'll discuss more later. However, let's talk about pricing now.

MRS. TELLER: Yes. That's what's most important to me.

COMMENTARY: *Exactly. The pricing is most important to Mrs. Teller, so talk about this in the beginning or you will lose her interest and she will lose her patience with you. You want to lead the potential sellers through the listing and selling process with an organized step-by-step explanation and detailed marketing plan. They need to be made aware of what to expect so they can decide if they want to sell their home.*

GINA: You may recognize some of the neighborhood houses I'm showing you. I included all of the homes on the market within a five-block radius with similar square footage, bedroom and bath count, and lot size.

MRS. TELLER: I'm sure that none of them are as nice as our house. We're the only custom-built home in the neighborhood.

GINA: That's a good point. I'm sure with your special touches none of the homes are as warm and inviting as yours. However, after a little research I found a few other homes similar to yours, one of which is currently on the market and one that recently sold.

COMMENTARY: *Show them the informational sheets, and if you need to you can go over it again at another time. You don't want to make the sellers feel like you're trying too hard to get them to agree with you.*

GINA: You have a wonderful home, and I'll be sure to point out every detail to potential buyers. For example, your kitchen layout, with all that counter space and those beautiful knotty pine cabinets, is very desirable.

COMMENTARY: *Start going through the comparable homes and their qualities. Change the energy of the conversation by picking up the pace.*

GINA: The very first comparable house on the market has a smaller kitchen, which could be expanded, and the yard is very large. It is currently listed for $369,000.

MRS. TELLER: We won't take that. We won't sell for less than . . .

COMMENTARY: *Let the sellers talk. Listen to their comments and give them more information that will help them in the selling process. They are nervous. Give them confidence.*

GINA: Remember, we decided that we'd wait until we reviewed the information and then talk about it.

MR. TELLER: Yes, Edith, that's right.

COMMENTARY: *Now you are leading. Slowly, go through the rest of the comparables and prices so they understand. Point out the important pros and cons of their property compared to others. Discuss the features of their house relative to those you've seen in comparable homes. Is their kitchen larger or smaller? Are the baths more or less updated than in other homes in the area?*

GINA: It's great that you received my mailer for the Mosers' house. I'd like to talk to you a little bit more about my marketing plan and strategy for selling your home. My goal is to expose your property to the greatest number of potential buyers. By doing this, I believe you'll get the highest price in the least amount of time, and I can make it a pleasant experience for you both.

As I mentioned before, one of the many marketing tools that I like to employ is to use the Internet to show off properties. And with a home as lovely as yours, it would be the perfect tool. That way, potential buyers can view your home at any time. I also like to advertise in the city newspaper and smaller area papers. It's important to reach out to as many potential buyers as possible, and some buyers prefer print ads to using a computer.

COMMENTARY: *Emphasize the way some buyers like to view and research properties. Don't forget to mention newspapers and advertising. Acknowledge the fact that some sellers aren't used to computers. Don't assume that they have a computer or are computer literate.*

GINA: Now that we've had a chance to go over the prices in the neighborhood and the marketing plan, let's decide on a price for your home.

COMMENTARY: *Look at both sellers, but focus on Mrs. Teller, as she is probably the final decision maker.*

MRS. TELLER: Please tell us what you are thinking. I'm sure that you don't feel our house is worth as much as I do, but I'm curious to hear what you have to say.

COMMENTARY: *She's come around to consider your opinion. She is asking for direction, or she wouldn't have asked you.*

GINA: I truly like your house. You have given it a homey feel that I believe most people would respond to instantly. You've maintained it and kept it in tip-top condition. The original features are of good quality and in terrific condition.

COMMENTARY: *Continue and make sure that Mrs. Teller is listening to you. It is important to maintain eye contact at this moment. She may not be thrilled with what you will say, but after all, moving after raising her child and living in her home for forty-five years may not be easy for her. Be patient.*

GINA: I believe that the asking price for your home should be $380,000.

COMMENTARY: *Let them digest what you have said. You have demonstrated the value to them. Now let them think about it.*

MRS. TELLER: If that's the price you feel is correct, then our house would only be priced $5,000 over the price of the most recent sale just across the street. Since I feel that our house is superior to that one, it seems we should leave room for the buyer to negotiate. I want you to know if I agree to that price, I expect to get it.

GINA: If we agree to that price, I promise you, Mr. and Mrs. Teller, that I will work as diligently as possible to achieve it.

Showing the Tellers' Home

Congratulations! You got the listing for Mr. and Mrs. Teller's home. The post sign is in the front yard with your name on it. Your listing is published in your local newspaper or in the local multiple listing service in your area and perhaps on Realtor.com. Maybe you've created a flyer with photos of the property and highlights of the home. You receive your first call from an agent to set up an appointment to show the property. You call the Tellers and ask them if they'll agree to a three o'clock showing for the next day. Explain to them that buyers are not comfortable when sellers are present for showings and it really would be better if they were not home.

You want to make sure that you have plenty of time before the actual showing time to set up the house, turn on the lights, open the drapes, and straighten up if necessary. Hopefully an organized seller like Mrs. Teller will have everything looking nice and tidy for you to show the buyers, and you won't have to vacuum and do their dishes like I did when I first started out.

When the buyer's agent, in many markets also referred to as the selling agent, arrives with clients, be energetic, knowledgeable, and genuinely proud to represent the property. Point out the features and strong points, but allow the home to sell itself. Many times buyers know what they're looking for. Don't talk too much! The conversation may go something like this:

GINA: Hi, welcome. I'm Gina Simmons, the listing agent.

SELLING AGENT: I'm Lori Barker, and these are my clients, Sue and Jeff Thurman.

GINA: And who's that?

COMMENTARY: *Jeff Thurman is carrying a baby in his arms. They are clearly a family.*

SUE THURMAN: This is Jeff junior.

COMMENTARY: *This is a potential "ah-ha" moment for you. You'll want to make sure to point out the family attributes of the home.*

GINA: Jeff's room is ready for him. It even has a big *J* on the door. The sellers have a son named Jason who is now grown. They still have the *J* on the door from when he was a Little Leaguer. You'll see his baseball trophies are still there.

COMMENTARY: *Try to establish a friendly rapport with the buyers. The selling agent is looking for you to take the lead during the showing.*

SUE THURMAN: This home has three bedrooms and two bathrooms, right?

SELLING AGENT: Right. This is the one I told you about that just came on the market. I thought it would be perfect for you.

SUE THURMAN: We've seen so many homes over the last few months that it's hard to distinguish one from another at times.

GINA: We did just put this home on the market, and you're the first to see it. Lori called me as soon as it went in the multiple listing service. You're in good hands with her. She's definitely on top of things.

COMMENTARY: *Take the time to confirm your rapport with the other agent. Remember, the other agent will be your partner should you end up in a transaction. It will also show the clients that as agents you can work together, and it gives them confidence in you.*

GINA: Let me take you through the house.

COMMENTARY: *Hand the agent and the clients informa-tion sheets and flyers. Make sure to have copies for both.*

GINA: This will be helpful to you in remembering all the features of this home. And may I say, there are quite a few! There are also photos posted on the Web. If you have any questions as we go through, don't hesitate to ask me.

JEFF THURMAN: Can we see the yard?

SUE THURMAN: I prefer to see the kitchen first.

SELLING AGENT: Let's just follow Gina; she knows the best way for us to see this home.

COMMENTARY: *This could be an important and interest-ing opportunity to observe the needs of the buyers as a couple. As the listing agent, when you take the buyers through the home, be aware of whether they are paying attention to you. If they're not, you may be talking too much. At that point, you need to enlist the help of the selling agent to get the buyers focused. If the selling agent doesn't respond, then you should conduct the showing in the way that best highlights the features of the home. Try not to let the buyers wander around the house by themselves at first.*

GINA: As you can see, this house has a great floor plan. I'll just give you a quick tour, and then you can take your time and explore for yourself. The public rooms are well proportioned and lend themselves to entertaining. Before we get to the kitchen and the yard, I want to show you what I mean about how well the floor plan flows. Because the living room is a step down, it separates nicely from the dining room while allowing the light from this beautiful picture window to stream into the dining area.

SUE THURMAN: We don't entertain too much these days. It's hard with the baby.

SELLING AGENT: I remember the great dinner parties you've had and the food you made was unbelievable. I know that one day soon you'll be in the kitchen again, cooking up a storm.

GINA: Let's go to the kitchen now and see how you like it. The seller enjoys cooking and had the kitchen custom built with extra storage, a huge pantry, pullout drawers, and great counter space to work on.

COMMENTARY: *Don't say too much once you get in the kitchen. Observe the client taking in the space, and see if she or her agent opens any drawers or the pantry. If not, then quietly start to open the drawers and pantry to engage the client. The buyer's attention will ultimately move in that direction. If she's really interested in this home, she'll be more attentive; if not, she won't be. The yard is off the kitchen, and Jeff is staring out the kitchen window. Smile, walk over to the back door, and open it for him. This will signal him to go outside.*

GINA: Please, have a look at the yard.

JEFF THURMAN: It's a good yard. I can already envision playing catch with my son.

COMMENTARY: *They seem to be having mutual positive reactions to this home. Listen carefully.*

SUE THURMAN: Just hold off on buying that catcher's mitt. Could we see the bedrooms? How close is the master to the second bedroom?

GINA: The master bedroom is right next to Jeff junior's room. The third bedroom is on the other side of Jeff junior's room and shares a bath. The Tellers told me that when they had the home custom built, their son too was a baby, and they originally had a door connecting the bedrooms. They drywalled over it when their son was in junior high school. You could easily reopen it if that is important to you.

COMMENTARY: *Try to anticipate what might be important to the buyers during the showing. You need to listen carefully to what they ask and concerns that they express. If they don't really seem to like the house, don't jump in and offer information that won't be important to them.*

SELLING AGENT: Why are the sellers moving?

GINA: To be closer to their son and grandchildren. Otherwise, they really love their home and probably would never think of moving. They've maintained the house well, and they love the neighborhood and their neighbors.

SELLING AGENT: So, Sue and Jeff, do either of you have any questions for Gina?

SUE THURMAN: How's the plumbing and electrical? Do you know how old the roof is or if they've had any leaks?

GINA: Once you have an inspection, your inspector will be able to tell you about the condition of the systems. The Tellers did tell me that they put on a new roof about ten years ago. Mrs. Teller showed me the paperwork and the warranty when I signed the listing.

SUE THURMAN: She sounds thorough, like my mother.

JEFF THURMAN: And just like you.

COMMENTARY: *It's beginning to feel like this family could be the perfect match for this home.*

GINA: Please take as much time as you'd like to go back through the house, and let me know if you have any other questions. I'll be open on Sunday from one to four if you'd like to come back. Or if you'd like to come sooner, just have Lori give me a call. Thank you for the showing. It was a pleasure meeting you.

COMMENTARY: *When you finally have your first listing, you'll need to figure out the sellers' schedule so you can show the house to real estate agents and prospective buyers. While you may have initially thought the sellers wanted to sell their home, they may have a change of heart once you are indeed attempting to sell it. If you find it difficult to get your sellers to call you back to make an appointment for a showing, it's not a good sign. If your sellers will allow you to have a key to show their home, it will make a huge difference in making it convenient for agents or prospective buyers. Make your listings easily available to see so agents can depend upon showing them to their buyers.*

Many times at showings, you'll see some strange things. Remember you are inside people's personal lives, and at times, you want to laugh or scream. One seller I represented was an older man from a foreign country. He was very proud of his heritage and had many photo albums to show to anyone who was interested. He kept a huge photo album by the front door and wanted to show everyone who visited him the photos of his life. Many of the photos were very offensive. So I put the book in a closet in the kitchen. Understand, this book was so large and weighed so much that it was not easy for me to move around. Almost always, when I had showings at his home, he was cranky and would tell me not to move his book. Many times he would call me up hysterical after showings and would tell me that I'd always done something not to his liking during a previous appointment. It wasn't personal, he just didn't trust anyone at this late stage of his life. All I could do was comfort him so I could do my job and sell his house. Not all sellers are as accommodating as the Tellers.

Now that you're on your way to making commissions, you should learn what to do with your hard-earned money. This will include how to budget it, reinvest it in your business, and invest it wisely in your future.

You must learn to be still in the midst of activity and to be vibrantly alive in response.

—INDIRA GANDHI

CHAPTER SEVEN

Using Your Time and Money

People choose to go into the real estate business for various reasons. There are those who think it will be fun, others who see the industry as a way to build wealth and financial stability. Lastly, there are those who want to help people realize the American dream of owning a home. Whatever the reason, it is fair to say that if you are consistent, diligent, and serious about having a career in real estate, there is unlimited opportunity to make large sums of money through commissions. However, it is important to manage your financial matters and affairs properly so you can save some of your hard-earned dollars throughout your career. Financial independence is created by managing your money so that one day you will be able to enjoy the freedom and lifestyle that you have dreamed about. This chapter is about using your money and resources wisely.

When beginning a new retail business, you need things like inventory, equipment, a store or a facility from which to work. In real estate, all you need for start-up materials are a car, a computer, and a phone. You can begin in real estate easily with the things you most likely already own. You won't have a huge overhead for a long time, if ever. When I first started my real estate career, I used to work from my car. Since I spent most of the day driving around looking for business opportunities, I kept all of my files in the trunk. Eventually, I traded in my broken-down Volkswagen for a better car, and my windowless office for an entire suite of offices. I did that by putting in the time it took to earn both.

The most important investment you will ever make in your real estate career is the time you give to it each and every day. Every day you design the way you are going to learn your marketplace. You will need to be very knowledgeable about the properties that are for sale and those that have already sold. You will also need to know the demographics of different areas. What are first-time buyers looking for in a neighborhood?

Maybe long-time owners are looking to downsize and are ready to sell their home. Knowing your marketplace takes time to understand, and spending that time will be a great investment.

At times, I've had clients begrudge paying me a commission. Most buyers and sellers don't have any idea of the time commitment it takes to stay on top of the ever-changing marketplace. When I explain that I receive and respond to more than one hundred phone calls per day, nearly two hundred e-mails, and drive for more than four hours each day, it doesn't impress them; their only concern is buying or selling a house. Since your clients can't see the efforts you are making for them each day, you need to communicate with them on a regular basis. Communicating with your clients regularly is a big part of your time commitment. I promise you, the investment in time that you put into being the real estate expert, and using that expertise on behalf of your clients, will pay off.

Independent Contractor

A real estate agent is an independent contractor. The definition of an independent contractor is one who maintains independent control of one's business work schedules, accounting, and all other activities associated with operating a business. That means that you will have to be self-motivated and creative. There won't be anyone to tell you how many hours to work or what elements of your business to address during those hours. The "contractor" portion refers to some type of written agreement or contract executed between the independent contractor and the company or person who is hiring them to perform a job. In this case, it refers to the written agreement between you and your broker.

As an independent contractor, you have the opportunity to realize unlimited income from your hard work. As a result, there are also no financial guarantees. You are both the employee and the boss of your business; you are responsible for doing all the work to build it and operate it. You set the parameters for your success. As you create your work environment, your future will unfold before you. As you build your business with positive energy, you will be full of new and exciting ideas. Here's where your multitasking skills will be challenged, because you will be making and executing all of the decisions. So, stay focused and move forward with enthusiasm in an organized fashion. This will help you accomplish a multitude of things at the same time. It will be helpful to you to use your vision board. You are in charge; you are responsible and accountable to yourself to make your dreams come true.

My suggestion is that at this stage, you should have put an ending time to your day. As mentioned in chapter 3, by doing this, you will increase the productivity of your work day, because all the things you need to accomplish have to get done by the scheduled end time you set for yourself. You will need to learn to determine your own style regarding how you accomplish your work schedule.

Being an independent contractor does provide a wonderful sense of freedom. It can be scary too, because of the realities of the self-imposed discipline and responsibilities. You will experience some of those realities, such as paying your own income taxes, all personal and business expenses, and insurance, and all the while keeping to your schedule.

Remember, as an independent contractor, you are your business. The choices you make in your real estate relationships with your fellow agents will outlive many of the relationships you will have with your buyers and sellers. We have a saying in the real estate business that buyers and sellers come and go, but we have one another to deal with for years. You must always do the right thing. These relationships will become one of your most valuable resources.

Desperate People Do Desperate Things

There will be times when interacting with different people in real estate that your normal voice will be desperate to roar. No matter how you feel, don't ever say bad things about another agent. Putting your fellow agents down will only serve to make you look bad. You don't want to be the bearer of bad news. Don't listen to gossip or repeat stories about others.

One day I was on my way to a listing appointment to meet with a seller about representing his home. I was running slightly early and arrived to find the front door open. The seller was honest with me when he set up the appointment, telling me he would be interviewing other agents as well. He told me if I arrived and he was busy with someone else to go ahead and look around the house. It was a three-level house, so I opened the door while hearing distant voices and turned down the hallway. All of a sudden I heard my name mentioned. I stopped walking for a moment and could hear the seller saying to the other agents that he was going to interview me next. The next voices I heard were saying awful things about me, and I was standing there listening! I couldn't believe my ears, my heart was racing. Unfortunately,

I didn't count to ten. I sprang down the stairs to where they were standing.

My presence took everyone by surprise. I think we all gaped in horror. I asked the other agents why they needed to say mean things about me. I looked them in the eyes and then at the seller of the property, apologizing for this unfortunate confrontation and the agents' lack of professionalism.

Later that day, the agents came to me to apologize and told me they were desperate to get that listing and they didn't mean what they had said about me. Although I did forgive them, and we have continued working professionally together at times, to this day I have not forgotten. In my opinion they crossed the line of professional and ethical behavior and called it desperation as an excuse.

You will experience human behavior at its finest and at its worst in the real estate world. Stay on your own path and don't be swept into the drama that may present itself. I truly believe in all the clichés you have heard in life: honesty is the best policy, good will overpower evil, what goes around comes around, do unto others as you would have them do unto you, truth is the best medicine, don't run from the truth. If you think about it, you most likely could add a few clichés to this line of thinking.

I want to emphasize the importance of this chapter, not only for your successful real estate career, but as a course of behavior to follow for the rest of your life. Always hold your head high. Be proud of your character, and integrity, and the way you have chosen to live your life. Just ignore the negative flags waving at you. I never once compromised my values, no matter how much I wanted or needed a commission check. Yes, there were times I was desperate to make ends meet, but I refused to do desperate things to make that happen.

Today I have a wonderful, loyal clientele, the respect of my fellow real estate professionals, my daughter, and my self-respect. I wouldn't trade this for all the tea in China, as my mother would say. It is important to try to stay away from people who are less scrupulous in their dealings. After all, you need to maintain your integrity to maintain longevity in the real estate profession.

Reputation

As you grow in life, you will experience many changes along the way as you adapt to building your business. Do not underestimate the importance of a good reputation. A good reputation will be a gratifying resource for you. Clients and agents will want to do business with you because you are well respected. At times, you may be challenged as to your belief system and code of ethics. Business adjustments are a normal part of growth. When confronted with situations that require your personal compromise, it's a red flag. I have often asked people what they do when they are driving and see a flashing yellow light, which indicates caution, slow down. Do you adhere to the warning, or do you step on the gas to get through the traffic light quickly? This example is a metaphor for many choices that we make in life. Remember in chapter 1 when I saw Joe across the room and all of my personal signals alerted me that it was a bad situation? My internal yellow lights were screaming. Obviously my choice did not have a very good outcome. If you can learn from my example, perhaps you will take the time to review a questionable option before ignoring the warning signs.

Everyone has to make her own choices and live with them. However, in the pursuit of happiness and financial freedom, there really isn't a lot of leeway in the time it takes to recover to stay on a path to success. There will be times when people you do business with will ask you to do something that you know isn't right. You will know this because it is a fact, or because you feel it in your gut. When you feel this alarm inside you, pay attention.

I once knew an agent who ignored his internal warning. He had been holding an open house when one of the pipes in the bathroom burst. He promptly called a plumber, who fixed the water pipe. After the plumber left and the open house ended, the agent patched and repaired the wall himself. He was nervous. His listing was nearing the three-month mark, and despite all his efforts the house just wasn't selling. The agent was getting worried that the sellers might pull the listing from him and give it to another agent. It was a nice home; however, the market was a bit slow at the time. Unfortunately, the agent was in a financial bind at the time, so it was crucial to him that he sell this house.

One Sunday afternoon, an enthusiastic couple came to his open house. They fell in love with the home and wanted to buy it. The proper action at this point would have been for the agent to disclose the fact that the pipe had burst. But the agent needed the sale and couldn't afford to jeopardize it. So he didn't say anything. The buyers had their inspector come in, but their inspector didn't find the damage the busted pipe had caused. The agent still had time to disclose this issue, but he didn't. The transaction went through, the sellers bought the house, and the agent got his commission. Then the pipe burst. Ironically, the new owners happened to call the same plumber that the agent had called during the open house. The plumber told the new owners that he had been there a few months ago to fix the very same pipe. They were understandably enraged and rightly sued. The agent was found guilty of fraud and nondisclosure. He lost his license and paid a hefty fine. In the end, withholding the truth never serves anyone well.

Commission Structures

When you make your choice of a real estate brokerage office to work with, you will place your license with that office. They will be your broker. You will need to discuss with your broker a commission agreement that specifies how the commission is shared between you and your office. As you earn commissions, your check for each transaction will be determined by the formula that you and your broker negotiated: This will probably be your first negotiation. When commissions are paid to your brokerage company, the broker will then pay you according to the agreement you negotiated. Keep in mind that above and beyond your negotiated commission agreement, there may be additional fees you are required to pay to your brokerage company. Depending on the area, a company may have additional marketing, transactional, or insurance fees. So if you negotiated an arrangement of a 50-percent split of the commissions you earn, which is often the case for new agents, you may be taking home less than that amount.

Budgeting

Given the exciting, exhilarating, and unpredictable nature of the real estate business, you may be very busy one month and very slow the next. You have to be creative, self-motivated, and an out-of-the-box thinker and planner. You will need to create a budget for your business and your personal life. As you work on building your business, you won't necessarily be closing escrows and collecting commission checks regularly. But each work day, you will be laying the groundwork for future business.

As you budget yourself, it will be difficult to plan the exact commission dollars you will be earning. In the beginning there are some important things to consider. As you embark on your real estate career, do you have a source of income to sustain you financially while you build your business? Are you working part-time in another profession during the day or evenings? If you do have another job, you will not only need to budget your dollars, but you will need to budget your hours, too. In any event, you are going to need to figure out how much working capital you will have to get started in real estate, to support you and your efforts.

In chapter 2, I described how I had some cash from selling my jewelry that I kept in a bag in the bottom of my closet. This was my working capital. I made a list of the necessary living expenses I needed to pay, and I budgeted a small amount of money I could use to begin my real estate career. My budget ended up stretching for nine months until I made my first sale. In the beginning, as you develop your budget, it should not be based on counting on your commissions. One of the risks of being an independent contractor in real estate is that you may go for a long time without collecting a commission check.

I want to share with you now the financial realities of being an independent contractor. As you can see, you must think ahead now and have a strategy. It's important to learn how to budget for a minimum of one year without a commission check, which may mean stretching the dollars you do have a little further. A mistake many new agents make when they make their first few sales is that they immediately spend all of their money. This is not the way to budget yourself. As you close sales, remember to reinvest some money into your business so that it can grow. I recommend setting aside 10 percent of your commission check in a savings account, reinvesting 10 percent into your business, and putting aside 25 percent to cover your taxes. Give it some serious thought. Don't treat it lightly.

So, the first thing to do is to sit down and make two budgets, one for your personal life and another for your professional one. For your personal budget, include your fixed costs, those that you have on an ongoing basis, such as shelter, clothes, food, gas, electricity, phone, and car expenses. Consult with an accountant, who can tell you whether it's better for you to lease or own a car. You will have business expenses that are deductible from your taxes, such as your cell phone bill, computer, and technology expenses. Make sure to consult an accountant as well as the regulations governing the tax write-offs associated with these items. Also don't forget to schedule some time off, whether it's going to a movie or taking a vacation; the time and money for this should be in your budget as well. Don't do what I did and work for three years and nine months without a break.

Some things to consider for your business budget will be your real estate license fees and insurance. If you have a marketing campaign, don't forget to include costs, such as mailers and flyers. You must maintain a budget and monitor your spending in every area of your life. Be careful to not fall short with your finances. This will make you anxious and desperate to make a sale, which will cloud your judgment and affect your negotiation skills. When you start to guide your clients based on your needs, financial or otherwise, the outcome will not be favorable.

I've said it before, but it's important to say again: Don't forget to pay your taxes! As an independent contractor, you won't be receiving a W-2 as you would if you were salaried; instead, you will receive a 1099-misc form from your real estate brokerage company that will reflect the money you've earned that year.

Tracking Your Expenses

Now that you've created a budget, don't forget to keep track of your expenses. Make two lists, one for your personal expenses and the other for your business expenses. Open separate checking accounts for each, even if you have minimal amounts of money to deposit. It's important to establish the habits you will need to continue to develop as your business grows. When you combine your money in the same account, it makes it much more difficult for you to separate your business and personal expenses. When I first started my career, I had no guidance or business experience, and I knew nothing about accounting. Keeping my money in a bag in the bottom of my closet was really not a very effective accounting system. It took me years to establish professionally correct ways to account for my life and my business.

It would be very helpful to use an accounting software program. In my business I use a software program called Quicken. It works well for me because it tracks all of my business expenses and tracks monthly what I spend. Take the time to be aware of how much money it takes to run your life and your business. At one point in my career, someone pointed out to me that my business expenses were in fact 67 percent of my earnings. I was shocked to learn that I was overspending to that degree. I had to figure out what I was spending and if it was really necessary to the operation and growth of my business. Had I continued on that path, I would have ended up deeply in debt.

When you are an independent contractor, there is no precise way to predict your exact income. There may be periods of time when your commissions come all together in a flurry and others when you have no income coming in at all. That's why it's so critical that you budget your expenses and don't spend what you earn all at once. You can never be quite sure when your next commission check will arrive. There will be times when you've worked tirelessly trying to close a sale and at the last minute something goes wrong and one party cancels. This could be devastating, because you may have earmarked those funds for something important. We have all been in this situation. I can not emphasize enough how important it is to be aware of your finances! It is imperative that you learn to save some of your hard-earned commissions for future expenses. After all, we're being paid on a commission basis, which can be unpredictable at times.

Be smart about where and how you spend your hard-earned money. Analyze all expenses so they make sense and fit into your budget. If you are already a working real estate agent, look at your personal and professional expenses and compare them to your income. Where can you significantly reduce the debt in your life? I have seen many agents crippled under the pressure of their finances, so distraught that they could barely work. Remember what we discussed about attitude and positive thinking? Debt will undoubtedly challenge even the most positive person. Even though you may want to wish the debt away, it won't disappear. You have to take a stand, boldly face the choices you've made, and, if need be, make serious changes immediately. When my expenses reached close to 70 percent of my income, it was time for me to take a long, hard look at where, what, and how my money was being spent. It was at that same time that I learned how to budget for taxes.

Paying the Piper

I was behind on paying my taxes, and when I was ready to file my return, I was shocked to learn how much I owed. I was devastated by the thought of having to come up with so much money so quickly and all at once. I remember the woman's voice on the phone, my heart racing and tears streaming down my face. All I kept repeating to the voice at the other end of the phone was, "I'm a single mother; I'm sorry." I was working just to keep up with life's expenses, and now I was sitting at my desk trying to figure out how I was going to pay this debt. I'd never been an independent contractor before and didn't really grasp the full responsibility of being one. I did pay the debt that I owed. It took two years of the IRS garnishing my income from every commission I earned, and it was a huge wake-up call for me. It gave me the opportunity to rethink how I was running my business and my life. I had learned how to work in real estate; now I was learning how to work my business and how to budget and be accountable. Today, I have an organized system for my business and my life, and a budget that keeps me on track.

Spending Your Marketing Dollars Wisely

Along with a car, a computer, and a phone, you will need to think about other necessities to begin and grow your real estate practice. If you are representing sellers, they will probably want to know how you plan to sell their home. Perhaps they will ask you for a written marketing plan before they'll sign a listing agreement with you. There are many ways to advertise and market most homes without spending a lot of money, such as online venues. For example, Craigslist is an effective site where buyers look for real estate. There is no fee for posting your listings; however, you will need to repost them every week. In your local marketplace, there will be area mailers, newspapers, and all kinds of message posting boards available to you, such as Veterans of Foreign Wars (VFW) and college message boards, and radio as well as other media opportunities. Many of these marketing and advertising venues will cost a minimal amount of money. Research them and make a list of what you feel would best represent you in your marketplace. Be proactive and see where the seasoned agents are advertising. If you pay attention, you can learn a lot from their choices and experience. Another idea may be to print a color flyer of the property you want to sell and distribute it in as many places as possible, even your local grocery store. Of course, you will need to use your local multiple listing service and take advantage of your company's advertising opportunities.

If you are in a higher-end marketplace, your clients may expect a more polished presentation for their homes. The cost of marketing and advertising higher-end properties can be significantly higher than marketing a modest home. A one-page ad in a magazine can cost you several thousand dollars. Be sure that before you spend this amount of money that it is in the budget you have dedicated to marketing this type of property. Maybe you could have a discussion with your sellers and see if they will pay some of the related expenses. Perhaps some of these expenses could be reimbursed to you by the sellers when the house is sold.

If you follow our basic rule of reinvesting 10 percent of your commission check back into your business, you may have to juggle your finances and forego a few expenditures from time to time. Your biggest outlay is your time. How many hours do you spend with a seller or buyer? How much money do you spend advertising your listings and marketing yourself? Since you spend a lot of time and money up front, with no guarantee of a return, the answers to these questions may be tricky without a budget, a commonsense marketing approach, and a leap of faith.

If you know that your fixed monthly business expenses are one thousand dollars and a given sale will yield a gross commission of two thousand dollars, then you have a one thousand dollar budget to spend on that property. That amount has to include pay for the time and effort you spent on the sale. Even though you won't be out any money, you won't have increased your savings or your reinvestment accounts. What is the value of your time and effort? Maybe your time spent led to other sellers meeting you at open houses and resulted in listing appointments and other potential business. Maybe your buyers didn't find what they were hoping to purchase, but they were so impressed with you and the time you spent with them that they referred other business to you.

What if you spend a thousand dollars and the property doesn't sell? Well, that could happen, and you just have to be prepared and move on. Don't look back. Focus on the present with an eye on the future. Believe that you will make a sale every time you try and have a positive attitude. You have to have faith that if it doesn't work out this time, the next opportunity will yield a more favorable outcome. Maybe the next commission check you receive is five thousand dollars. You can then cover your monthly one thousand dollars in expenses and have four thousand dollars left. Maybe you only spent one thousand dollars marketing the next home and it sold quickly; then you will be three thousand dollars ahead as well as having expended fewer hours of your time.

The point is that your earnings and your expenses are unpredictable. So you need to plan ahead and have a reserve account so that when there is an opportunity to put more money into the budget, you can do so to cover unexpected expenses in the future. You should have an overall idea of how much money it takes to operate your business. Ideally, you would budget for the coming fiscal year during the last month of the preceding fiscal year. The earlier into the year you can figure out how to cover your fixed operating expenses, the better idea you will have about what marketing dollars are available for your properties and your personal needs. Always keep in mind that you have basic living expenses. In real estate, gas can be a big cost of doing business. Use common sense in terms of the expenditures on overpriced property and personal marketing campaigns. You know that the sale of a $300,000 home will be more profitable than the sale of a $150,000 home. However, you know that if you list a home for sale for $250,000 and the area average is $200,000, the marketing and advertising dollars associated with that listing may not yield a return because the property has been overpriced. Putting an individual marketing plan together for each listing is very important in order to understand where your marketing dollars are committed.

You have to start marketing yourself the minute you get your license. You have to order cards with your photo on them. Business cards with photos provide the client and your real estate agent peers with a constant reminder of your face and name. It also keeps you in the mind of future prospects. Many agents order company scratch pads or pens with their name and phone number on them. They give these as handouts at Sunday open houses and when door knocking. When showing properties to a buyer, include a scratch pad and pen in his packet of information; this will allow him to take notes on the various properties and is an easy way to market yourself. If you choose to send a mailer, make sure it reflects who you are and how you do business. It will be your calling card. In many instances, it will be the first introduction you make to potential buyers and sellers. You have to know your target audience and spend your dollars wisely. You want your potential clients to connect with who you are and make them feel as though you understand them and their interests.

Additionally, you need to be consistent with mailing. You can't mail one or two times and expect results. You must mail on a continual, scheduled basis. I've been mailing the same postcard every month for over twelve years: "Want Your Home Sold? Got Valerie?"

Your marketing plan should also include for sale signs. The signs should display your name and number clearly and should be placed in the front yards of homes you represent. Now you are marketing yourself as a listing agent. Not only will buyers see your sign and call for an appointment to see the house, but other sellers will call you to list their homes, as well.

Over the years I have attended many business seminars and listened to a variety of speakers and internationally renowned consultants. One of the most creative, insightful, and influential industry leaders I ever observed—and subsequently had the honor of knowing—is Allan Dalton. Allan at the time of this publication is the CEO of Realtor.com, and over the years our paths have crossed on numerous occasions. During his stellar career in the industry, he has created real estate marketing systems for Coldwell Banker, Century 21, ERA, and Better Homes and Gardens, to name only a few. His career includes twenty years as president and co-owner of a thirty-two-office real estate brokerage as well as being a senior executive of National Realty Trust (NRT), the company with which I am proudly associated. Allan is widely respected for his professional expertise and closely followed for his market insights. My interview with him, presented here, contains profound, practical ideas for veterans and new real estate agents alike.

VALERIE: What information do new real estate agents need to know when they're beginning a career in the real estate industry?

ALLAN: New real estate agents need to be clear regarding their career premise and motivation in order to begin formulating a sound strategy and business plan. Traditionally, the real estate industry has not attracted strategic-minded individuals. When I asked tens of thousands of agents across America, "How many of you had a plan or strategy that you would enter the real estate industry?" only a handful answered yes. I cannot imagine asking a similar number of doctors or lawyers the same question and not having almost all respond that they were currently living out their strategy.

VALERIE: What sort of strategy are you referring to?

ALLAN: I'm referring to the need for agents to be seriously and fully committed and engaged with their decision regarding real estate, as opposed to what I hear a lot of agents at career nights commenting: "I think I'm going to give real estate a try." I doubt very much that you would hear people say, "I'm going to try to be an attorney" or "I'm going to give medicine a try." This lack of strategic thinking, which leads to a less-engaged attitude about what one does, is also reflected in how often I hear real estate professionals, when asked, "What do you do for a living?" actually respond by saying "I'm in real estate, but I used to be a teacher" or "I'm in real estate, but I was with the government for twenty-five years." This example of how one is living in the past and not strategic about the future would be like someone saying, "I'd like you to meet my wife, Alice; and here's my ex-wife, Betty." Today's forward-thinking real estate agents determined to be successful need to realize that strategic thinking is pivotal for career success. Ironically, those entering new careers with firms like the IBMs of the world don't need to be strategic in their thinking, because the company has an overarching strategic vision for them to follow. In real estate, that's not true. Successful real estate professionals not only need to be strategic, they need to be creative thinkers to differentiate themselves in a highly competitive environment. I once read that only approximately 3 percent of the workforce have jobs that require creative thought, and that 97 percent of the workforce just process work the company asks of them. Valerie, you are a stellar example of how to blend business planning and creative thinking. Yes, if you were at IBM you could succeed without either, as long as you followed that particular corporation's recipe for success. But in real estate, you've got to create your own recipe.

VALERIE: And how would you suggest agents do this?

ALLAN: It begins with the understanding that every company and agent has to compete along two separate lines. I was once told by the dean of Stanford University's business school that to compete successfully, all companies and individuals need to develop both a positional and a capabilities advantage over their competitors. A positional advantage exists when a company like McDonald's establishes prime locations all over the world. A capabilities advantage exists when a company like Burger King opens across the street and offers breakfast when McDonald's does not. Given the increasingly competitive landscape that real estate agents are contending with, the need to compete successfully for both a positional and a capabilities advantage is more acute than ever. That's why it's important that every strategic-minded real estate agent looks to join a company that enjoys a positional advantage because of its brand as well as a capabilities advantage because of its systems and skill-development programs. One without the other is not enough. As important as it is for new agents to join companies that can provide them with these inherent advantages, it's equally important for the company to help new agents establish their own positional and capabilities advantages. New real estate agents would be well served by imitating you, Valerie, and the way you diligently worked to develop your own personal brand and name, as well as your career-long dedication to developing a skills-based capabilities advantage.

VALERIE: How do technology and the Internet play a role in an agent's success? How could an agent best use these resources as marketing tools?

ALLAN: Great question, Valerie. Let's revisit the premise of developing both a positional and a capabilities advantage. The Internet enables new agents to accelerate their timetable for success, because not all agents who enjoy a positional advantage developed over many years of personal brand building have also embraced and leveraged the unprecedented capabilities advantage the Internet can afford. The Internet transcends a lot of the relationships involving the more seasoned agents and companies, because today's customer begins his real estate search online. Therefore, every real estate agent and company is engaged, whether they know it or not, in an online battle to be the first point of consumer contact. Crudely put, successful real estate professionals know they need to be at the top of the food chain online. The need to be there at the beginning of the home search and to be available for any consumer's real estate related inquiry also supersedes the hackneyed industry cliché that real estate agents need to be at the center of the transaction. In fact, they now need to be involved before and after the transaction, as well as at the center, in order to maintain real estate relevance.

VALERIE: Having said that, when a new agent is asked by a potential client how she is different from her competition, what would you suggest she say?

ALLAN: Since a new agent cannot say, "I have twenty years' experience" or "I sold ten million dollars of real estate last year," she needs to express her value in a way that shifts the focus away from her modest track record and instead speaks to the dominant consumer needs that many more successful agents sometimes overlook.

VALERIE: Can you give me an example of how agents can communicate this to consumers?

ALLAN: Certainly. When asked by a home seller, "How are you different?" an agent could respond with the following: "Rather than focus on either how I'm different from other agents or how my company is different from other companies, I think it's more important to focus on how your property has to be viewed as being different, versus the other properties it will be in competition with in today's competitive marketplace. You see, Mr. and Mrs. Homeseller, I don't compete against other agents as much as your home competes with other properties for sale in this marketplace. In fact, I actually cooperate with the other real estate agents, but your home doesn't cooperate with the other properties for sale. Let me stress that point: your home competes; it doesn't cooperate. Therefore, the way that I strive to be different is to make sure that buyers understand how different and more desirable your home is. Specifically what I'd like to review with you this evening is my customized marketing plan to provide your property necessary differentiation, and it begins with the Internet."

VALERIE: Given your work with Realtor.com, I'm not surprised by how heavily you're focusing on the Internet. How much do you think the Internet helps real estate agents?

ALLAN: The Internet both giveth and taketh away. For example, up to 50 percent of e-mails sent to real estate professionals by consumers go unopened. Therefore, for these agents, the Internet is demonstrating unintentional ineptitude, incompetence, and it is hurting the nonresponsive real estate professional. Moreover, many real estate agents still don't add multiple photos and virtual tours to the properties they are marketing. The Internet therefore hurts the way in which they are perceived by Internet-inclined consumers. Conversely, for real estate agents who fully leverage the Internet for marketing real estate and themselves, as well as for instant communication, they've never looked better by way of comparison. Thus they have a capabilities advantage. And they've never been more successful. And Valerie, there's no greater example of an agent who satisfies the needs of customers and clients, both offline and online, in a professional and responsive way, than you. I understand from Betty Graham, the president of your company, that you answer at least two hundred calls and e-mails a day, which automatically sets you apart in the mind of the consumer.

VALERIE: I've heard you speak many times, and one of the valuable points that you address is the distinction between marketing "to" and marketing "for" real estate consumers. Could you explain this provocative distinction and how it translates into income for all real estate agents?

ALLAN: I respectfully recommend that each and every real estate professional, new and veteran alike, establish his own definition of what marketing means to him. My favorite definition—and one that has guided me throughout my career—is that marketing is first determining the unmet needs of the marketplace and then creating goods and services to respond to those needs effectively. Emerging out of that classical definition would be the premise of marketing "for." Marketing "for" means creating goods and services that do in fact live up to that definition by responding to consumer needs effectively. Conversely, marketing "to" would be so-called marketing ploys, which instead seek to satisfy personal needs and self-aggrandizement versus satisfying consumer needs. Prominent pre-Internet marketing tools such as refrigerator magnets, advertising on park benches, recipes, and all the rest, while all creating a nice touch and serving a purpose, do not respond to crucial real estate consumer needs or marketplace relevance. Classic marketing "for" examples would be providing marketplace intelligence and predictive data regarding where the market is headed in terms of trends, absorption rate studies, and other types of quantitative information that builders have utilized for years and that can also benefit regular consumers. Marketing "for" examples would also include the ways a real estate professional not only sells more homes but can also help consumers sell their homes for more through merchandising and staging.

VALERIE: Can you give me an example of real estate agents you have known who have made this transition to marketing "for"?

ALLAN: I can give you one humorous one, yet it's still instructive. I had an agent in Chicago come up to me recently and say, "Mr. Dalton, I'm no longer advertising on supermarket carriages. Instead, I'm sending out market trend reports with my picture attached. But the reason is not your 'marketing for' advice." I said, "Oh?" and he told me, "My twelve-year-old daughter started crying at dinner one night, and I asked her, 'Honey, what's wrong?' She said, 'Daddy, you know how your picture is on the carriages at the supermarket? I'm very proud of you, but the problem is that all my friends at school think you're missing.'"

VALERIE: But seriously, Allan—how can an agent best use her marketing dollars?

ALLAN: Understand that every property on the Internet is in competition with every other property. So you want to deploy your marketing dollars to give your properties better shelf positioning. As an agent, you want to align your finite marketing dollars strategically to promote both yourself and your properties simultaneously. Every home is a product; every home has to be merchandised. If some agent has only one picture of his property, you should have multiple pictures of your properties, which also allows you to have the property featured on your personal Web site on Realtor.com. If you see that an agent mails a postcard, you can trump him by mailing a brochure. But don't do it because you're competing against the agent. Do it because your property is competing against his property. That's a "marketing for" spirit of intent. Seventy-five percent of the buyers in many markets come from within a fifty-mile radius. By mailing a brochure, you create the possibility of getting more listings in the areas to which you've mailed. You want to ask yourself this question: If I want to get multiple listings from the homeowners in the community, would they be more impressed if I spend my marketing dollars promoting properties or would they be more impressed if I'm advertising on a park bench saying how great I am? That's why it's important for an agent to look for ways to leverage her marketing, to create synergies and efficiencies by having multifunctional marketing.

VALERIE: It's great to learn how to market to general consumers from someone like you. Now how would you suggest real estate agents should market so other brokers are familiar with them and their properties for sale?

ALLAN: You need to market to and network with other agents, especially since the real estate community controls 99 percent of the buyers. You want to cooperate with the real estate community so when agents are working with their buyers, they will want to do business with you. Because every transaction has two sides, you want to create great relationships with other agents and be approachable. You don't want other agents being fearful of bringing their buyers and working with you in a transaction. If they think you're going to be unpleasant or that you don't wish them well, you are going to preempt cooperation, which hurts your clients. But if you are perceived as an agent who is respected within the real estate community, then other agents are going to want to work with you. If you will forgive the cliché, it takes two to tango. You have to make sure that you don't disenfranchise the other agents by making them look unprofessional in front of their clients. You want to market yourself so that it almost gets to the point where other agents are excited about working with you. This is part of learn-

ing your skill set, being a fierce negotiator for your clients while not being a predator in the eyes of the other
agents and their clients.

VALERIE: At your seminars, you talk about the difference between merely selling a home and selling a
home for more. Please share that with my readers.

ALLAN: The difference between selling a home and
selling a home for more is the difference between
simply listing the home and actively marketing the
home.

VALERIE: What exactly do you mean by that?

ALLAN: An agent representing the homeowner should
not just be in the role of selling the home. They
should put themselves in the role of marketing the
home by outdoing the competition and leveraging
the laws of supply and demand. For example, if you
had a pair of Super Bowl tickets, I could say, "Hey, let
me sell them for you. I'll get someone to buy those
tickets for three hundred dollars, which is what you
paid for them." But you probably don't want to sell
those tickets for three hundred dollars. You want to
sell them for more. Thus, you want to market them.
So you might want to work with someone different,
someone who is going to let all the corporate CEOs
know that you've got two Super Bowl tickets, which
may result in your selling them for ten thousand dollars! The difference is when you merely sell a home,

you sell it to a buyer. When you market a home, you get it sold to the right buyer by leveraging the laws of supply and demand. You create competition among eager buyers for that property, and that's what a capabilities-based marketing real estate agent can do.

VALERIE: That's a great point, but how would a real estate agent implement that strategy?

ALLAN: Think of it. A homeowner can sell his own home, but traditionally he can't sell his home for more because he doesn't have thousands of real estate agents, controlling 99 percent of the buyers, creating competition for his property. That's why people use real estate agents to market their homes— to get more. It's like the old philosophical question: "If a tree falls in the forest and no one is there to hear it, does it make a sound?" If a home is on the market but agents don't know about it, and therefore buyers don't know about it, then is it really on the market? The responsibility of the marketing agent is creating competition for the property. You create competition by giving the property exposure. On Realtor.com, properties that have multiple photos get approximately 300 percent more exposure than properties with one photo. If one hundred people are competing for one home, then that home goes up in value. The real estate agent is responsible for creating and managing buyer competition. And no one does that better than you, Valerie.

VALERIE: As you know, I am open to and embrace all of today's technology. It is important to keep the consumer's interest in mind when marketing. Having said that, may I ask what are the top five marketing tips you can give to a new agent?

ALLAN: These five undoubtedly are the most important:

1. Attach your personal promotion to the promotions that are important to the consumer. If I were marketing "for" real estate in Denver, Colorado, I would say something like, "Dalton Markets America's #1 Lifestyle: Denver." Then all the metropolitan residents of Denver would see that I am not just marketing myself or one single property. Instead, I'm painting on a larger marketing canvas. The more that people appreciate the value of Denver, the higher the value of every property being marketed in Denver. Future clients are able to see that you are marketing something that is directly tied into their greatest asset: their home. In essence, you are taking the entire community public. Therefore, the entire community will respond to your leadership regarding real estate.

2. Attach your significance to what is significant to consumers. If you are doing personal promotion and you mention how many homes you have sold, you may want to say something like, "I sell

so many homes because my clients deserve the very best." Your efforts should be for a consumer cause rather than self-aggrandizement. It's like agents who put on the back of their cards "The finest compliment I can receive is your referrals." That's about them. It should read "My greatest privilege is serving the real estate needs of you, your family, and your friends." Now the focus is on the consumer.

3. Do whatever you can to be a community-based real estate agent who coordinates the consumer's business and social networking sites—all under your leadership. For example, post your listings on the ever-growing national and international websites. This is but one way to show your sellers that you are reaching out to the global market on their behalf.

4. Marketing on the Internet, in and of itself, is not the whole answer. It is important to integrate your off-line and online marketing to appeal to the consumer's needs. Even though I've read that 82 percent of consumers go to the Internet first, research indicates that only about 16 percent use their Internet search to select the agent who will market their home. To boost your visibility, attend real estate and marketing seminars and consider giving local real estate seminars for your community.

5. Your marketing should reflect that you have evolved from just being in the service sector to being in the skill sector. Too many real estate professionals try to justify their value by simply claiming that they give good service, which is very difficult to quantify. Your skills as a real estate professional are extremely valuable and include negotiating, marketing, merchandising, and networking. Remember, you're worth far more as a skilled professional who gives great service than as a service professional with some skills.

VALERIE: If you could give one piece of advice to a new agent entering the real estate industry to carry her through her career, what would it be?

ALLAN: The most important information that I can give is that you need to gravitate to top producers in the industry. Look for mentoring, coaching, consider joining a team, get help with business planning. Equally vital, you must always believe in yourself. Please remember the old adage: "If you don't believe in yourself, that makes it unanimous."

The Truth Is

The truth is, the greatest factor that keeps us in our profession is the reward of feeling that we make a significant difference in people's lives. Most of our time when we encounter people in the real estate world, they are going through transitions, whether it's someone buying his first home, a family searching for more space, parents whose children have grown, aging adults who are retiring, or situations involving death and divorce.

Every time, in every situation, we listen to clients' needs and concerns and empathize with their plight, working as a team to fulfill their life requirements. Many times I have smiled and said, "Don't worry, I'm on your team, even if we grow old together." People may feel lonely and isolated during these times of transition. Letting them know you care is priceless.

Giving Back

I firmly believe in giving back to your community.

In my heart, I feel this should be a requirement of every real estate agent. You probably already do this without realizing it. If you have aging parents, you visit them and help make them feel a part of the world around them. If you have children, you may do what I did and help out at their school for special events, be the class mom, and drive them to sporting events. As you give, you will get back. Whether it feeds your soul doing good things for family and friends or helping people you have never met before, you may even meet a potential buyer or seller along the way. No matter what, you will meet like-minded people and have a great time doing it.

When I first started my career in real estate, time was the one thing I did not have enough of. As the years went by, my time constraints increased. Like most people, I had my head down, focused on work and family. When charitable opportunities arose, I would donate whatever money I could. However, I did not go out looking for charitable organizations to donate to, much less help found one of my own.

I had been in the industry for a little over eight years when my friend, Karen, who was into philanthropic endeavors, called and told me about an experience she had volunteering at a homeless shelter. She had accompanied a friend doing community service. While there, she met a five-year-old girl who slept on a cot in the shelter's kitchen. This beautiful little girl had sores all over her body from sleeping in the same clothes night after night; she was afraid to take them off for fear they'd be stolen. Karen was taken by the little girl and was appalled by the awful conditions under which she was living. She returned to visit the little girl, but she had been moved to another shelter. Many times children are moved around from shelter to shelter to keep them safe from an abusive parent or because there simply isn't enough room left for them. Karen was very upset and worried. She was passionate about helping this child. I listened and felt a pain in my heart from this story, especially since I had a daughter of my own. I expressed my concerns for the little girl, tried to put my friend's mind at ease, and tried to figure out ways to help her find a solution. Eventually, during that conversation, I reflected on my life, my time constraints, and personal concerns. Karen listened to what I had to say, paused, then said, "Well, don't you think we should do something?" I may have thought about taking action, but I didn't know what that action would be until she asked me this question. She was right; I did think I should do something. I had felt the instinct so many times, but I had stifled it with the day-to-day business of my own life.

I knew there would always be things that needed to be tended to and my time would always be in short supply. This little girl needed help right then, and my busy schedule needed to be put in perspective.

We borrowed a small office and called friends who were professional women who might be available to make a difference. We met many nights after feeding our children and putting them to bed. Those evenings were spent in a room with canary-yellow walls, brainstorming around a table covered with half-finished cans of Diet Coke. We started off by getting a merchant to donate duffle bags to us. We then bought school supplies, shampoo, and soap to fill the bags, which we then gave to the children. But we knew just giving them things was not enough; these children needed people to spend time with them. When a child knows you care about her, something in her changes.

Eight years ago, the women I joined forces with founded Children Uniting Nations. This nonprofit offers relationship-based academic and personal mentoring for children from foster care, group homes, and homeless shelters. We began with five hundred children from various state and local facilities. Eight years later, we have helped thirty-five hundred children, many of whom have gone on to find permanent or adoptive homes. And the little girl? She was adopted by my friend and is now attending college.

That experience awakened my concern for young girls and women. To my surprise, I was honored in 2001 with the Woman of Achievement Award from the professional board of the Big Sisters organization. I was just doing what I believed should be done; winning an award for it was not something I had ever imagined. Seeing the difference we can make in a child's life is the reward. Sometimes, I think it is the children who should be receiving awards for their bravery and trust in forging relationships with us. I am grateful whenever I can contribute to helping them.

One of my earliest lessons about giving back to young girls I learned at my daughter's sixth-grade graduation. As a parent in the audience watching the graduation video, I was surprised when ten out of the twenty girls on the video said they wanted to be real estate agents when they grew up. Little did I know, all those years that I had taken Vanessa and her little friends with me to showings and listings had made a lasting impression on them. You never know how you can affect one person's life. I was so proud to hear that these girls enjoyed their adventures with me and that it inspired them in ways I never knew.

Now that you have an earning capacity and a generous giving spirit, it's time to focus on managing your money and wealth building in your personal and professional life. The following chapter will help simplify your thinking of worth and worthiness. You can have it all!

You make a living by what you get,
but you make a life by what you give.

—WINSTON CHURCHILL

CHAPTER EIGHT

Your Worth

Whether you are making the big bucks or just starting out in real estate, you probably do have a net worth to begin your financial planning, unless you are a young person just starting out who may not have had the time to acquire the assets that create a net worth. For many young professionals, the debts they owe, like student loans, outweigh their assets. This is understandable and can be managed even when building a business.

To figure out your net worth, take a pen and a sheet of paper and draw a line down the middle. Title one side of the list Assets. Under this heading, write down all of the things that you currently own. Depending on where you are at this moment in your life, the items on your list will vary. Remember, this is an exercise. Whether you have a little or a lot is not the point. The point is to know where you are starting from so that you can build from there. A list may look like this:

Car

Jewelry

Equipment (stereo, computer, etc.)

Collections (art, stamps, coins, etc.)

Property

Cash Investments (stocks, bonds, etc.)

Title the opposite side of the page Liabilities. The liability column shows what you owe in credit card debt, student loans, and so forth. This may make you feel like sticking your head in the sand, because listing your assets may have made you feel rich. The liabilities column is the moment of truth that will enable you to understand exactly where you stand financially. Choosing to not be truthful with yourself about your net worth and financial situation will stop you from moving forward. So come on, be honest!

When you are finished listing your assets and liabilities, you will have a clear understanding of your net worth. It may be good news or bad news. Remember, it's just the news. The important thing is where you go from here. In this chapter we will discuss the basics of wealth building and personal investments. It's simpler than you think.

Creating Wealth

As women, we are well aware of our buying power. Fifty-five million strong, women between the ages of twenty-four and fifty-four drive the American economy, though it isn't until we look at actual numbers that we can see just how much we're spending. According to statistics American women control or influence $7 trillion in consumer spending a year! We are the target audience for commercials, print advertisements, and infomercials and make 80 percent of household decisions. Yet what we aren't well aware of is how to restrain our spending to empower ourselves to create a solid financial foundation. There is no security equal to knowing that you are able to care for yourself and your children financially.

So how can we harness the power of financial investments to best serve our future? What exactly is financial investment? To help you learn more about women's untapped power and find ways of building financial security and wealth management, I have interviewed Libbie Agran, president and chief investment officer of Libbie Agran Financial Services. She has thirty-eight years of experience in investment portfolio design and management. Libbie has taught national seminars and classes on a variety of financial topics and has lectured for *Money* magazine, various professional organizations, and corporations. Libbie is truly a trailblazer. Before founding her own firm in 1971, she worked as a systems engineer for IBM and a business manager for the University of California Statewide Extension.

VALERIE: There is the potential for women to learn a great deal from one another. We've talked a lot about the importance of having a mentor to help your business grow. Did you have a mentor?

LIBBIE: I have had many mentors. My first mentor was a woman who deeply believed in me named Lucille Simon. She was married to the industrialist Norton Simon. Together they started a company called Hunt Foods and later went on to build an empire that included Avis, Canada Dry, and other companies. In 1970 Lucille lost her eyesight to sudden-onset glaucoma, and around this same time, she and Norton divorced and Lucille's life changed dramatically. Since Lucille and Norton had developed a strong financial partnership, she felt overwhelmed by having to manage her financial life alone. She asked me to work with her to develop a financial strategy, since I was already managing government grants portfolios in the office of Economic Opportunity, funded through the University of California. As we worked together, she constantly questioned her own attitudes as a single woman with wealth. I shared with her my desire to educate and empower women to build wealth and bring about social change. I had been working with her for a year when she said to me, "You have an idea here. Let's talk about how we can do this for more women than just me." So she was the one who really encouraged me. She was a very important mentor. She helped me finance some of the studies I did about women and money. She believed in me until the day she died, which was about ten years ago.

VALERIE: You mentioned that you didn't have only one mentor. Most people are lucky if they even have one. Who was your other mentor?

LIBBIE: The other person was my grandmother. My grandmother was four foot nine, and she was really a tiny dynamo. She didn't know a thing about finances, but she had left a very secure home to marry a mining engineer in 1910. She had been a lovely lady with white gloves when she went out west. She became a pioneer, living in mining towns with my grandfather. There she learned everything: how to rope horses, how to ride horses, and how to deliver babies.

She would always say, "There is nothing in this world that you cannot do. Don't ever let anyone tell you that you can't do something. You can do it." That relationship was extremely important to me because she mentored me and my girlfriends and yet she ended up poor.

She ran out of money because she ended up living until the age of ninety-five. A lot of our discussions the last twenty-five years of her life were, "What could I have done differently to have not ended up with nothing?" Fortunately, living with my husband and me the last few decades of her life, she escaped the fear that many women, both then and now have; ending up poor and alone.

Many women who lived through the Great Depression outlived their husbands only to end up penniless. It really made me think a lot about women. Watching her and taking care of her I decided I never wanted to see another woman in that position again. It was really hard for her to live, as she said, "thanks to graciousness of others."

With Lucille having tons of money but feeling helpless because of her illness, and my ninety-five-year-old grandmother feeling helpless because she ran out of money, I realized the vulnerability that women can face.

VALERIE: We continually see how having a mentor or mentors and creating a support structure for yourself can help motivate us and propel us forward. How does having a mentor factor into creating a solid financial foundation?

LIBBIE: When I went into the field of life planning and portfolio management, there were only two other women in the field. It wasn't until I had made a name for myself, doing a lot of lecturing around the country, that I eventually met them and earned their respect. In the interim, finding role models and having a supportive group of friends around me were the two major steps to moving forward with my career. This is why I teach these steps in my economics of being a woman and wealth-management classes.

VALERIE: Why are these two steps important and in what ways?

LIBBIE: First of all, I believe that women do better if they have a variety of mentors and not necessarily just one. Having a mentor who you can interview for specific business skills to see how she was able to succeed is highly beneficial. Emulating women in the business world or in your field who you admire allows you to ramp up motivation in challenging moments. It's also important to share your fears and concerns with friends, to obtain the emotional support and encouragement you need and to check in repeatedly with your role models, because as you grow and change, so might they. You want to keep visualizing the successful person, the person you admire.

The second thing I think is extremely important, and that I talk a lot about with women today, is dreaming about your goals—writing them down on paper and just dreaming about what exactly you want for yourself. What do you want to do in the next month? What do you want to do in the next quarter, the next half year, and the next year? It's your brainstorming session. Don't worry about whether or not you can achieve goals A, B, or C; this exercise is about freeing yourself. Write those goals down, then go on to brainstorm and dream about what your goals are in two years, three years, five years, and then ten years. Sometimes it helps to do it with a friend. At this point you're not planning any financial strategy, you're just trying to get down on paper what's important to you. Talking those goals through with a friend helps to put them in the order of priority. Once you've done this—and it may take several go-rounds, whether alone or with other people—you can then move forward.

VALERIE: Do you feel that women are different from men when it comes to how we behave regarding money and finances?

LIBBIE: Yes, as women we are different. We talk, we share, and we network in a much more open way than men do. Most men are very competitive with money. They will boast about what they've done, but they will almost never ask for help or advice from another man. Women have the advantage of being able to talk to one another. That's why I think having women pick out the people whom they admire and then talking to those people to find out how they did it is the best way to approach learning about finance and wealth. I encourage women to come together in a group, even if it's just with three or four people, because then you start to hear other women's goals. You can sit down and talk about your own lifestyle and begin to ask questions of other women. What are you spending your money on? How have you been able to limit your spending? What are your goals? Knowledge and potential are there within each of us to build wealth, and it's important that we share what we know.

VALERIE: So if as women, we can put together a group of friends to discuss money issues, what would be the next step?

LIBBIE: From there you would begin to put a dollar amount toward your financial goals. Whether it's buying a car, buying a house, continuing education, or having a child—whatever that goal might be, there are financial considerations. All of this comes before the investing. If you don't do these exercises about what you really need in your life, and model yourself after people whom you admire who have become successful and have achieved things that you want, figuring out the financial aspects is much harder.

VALERIE: Let's say a group of women put together a financial women's group. Are there helpful Web sites you would recommend for them to visit for trusted information and ideas?

LIBBIE: Yes. You could organize meetings with your friends just like a book club. One person goes on the Internet and looks at www.money.cnn.com, and another one looks at www.motleyfool.com. Each person has an assignment to check out something specific and reports back each week. I try to get the women I'm teaching to go on the Web every day. I feel the most informative magazine to follow is *Kiplinger's Personal Finance*. I tell each of my students to subscribe to it. And then I tell them to go on the Web site, which is described in detail in the magazine.

Every month *Kiplinger's* will give you the best mutual funds to invest in, and it will tell you how to update your insurance. It's the most helpful and informative source in America, and most people don't even know about it. It has been around since 1947, and I have never found an error in the magazine. I have found it to be an invaluable tool for the beginner and seasoned investor. The magazine has a great advisory team making recommendations.

VALERIE: Can you recommend a simple way women can implement these ideas on a regular basis so that the ideas become a routine part of their lives?

LIBBIE: The simplest way to center your life on investing is to make a date to get together once a week with like minds who want to learn how to build their financial future. Once you have created a group and have done the research, try to develop your own personal plan on how to move forward in life financially.

VALERIE: What steps would you suggest for developing a personal plan?

LIBBIE: There are really three things that you have to think about: lifestyle, saving and investing. You must analyze your current lifestyle—what it costs in dollars. Then you can think about what you want your lifestyle to become. Building wealth and being successful as an independent woman involves understanding your lifestyle needs and knowing where you spend every penny. Sitting down to review your expenses is something you have to do every month. From there you will honestly see what your lifestyle costs you, you will establish your priorities, and you will know how much money you can save and invest.

VALERIE: How would you advise women to make this a habit in their daily lives?

LIBBIE: The next step might be making an appointment with yourself to review your expenses and investments every week, the way you make an appointment for exercise or anything else that is of importance to you. It's an action that has to be taught and repeated. It's important to take the time to practice good financial habits or there will be a strong possibility that you may arrive in a place in your life where you are without financial resources. Spending an hour and a half weekly, investigating and learning about financial markets can easily be worked into your schedule when viewed from this perspective.

VALERIE: Can you share with me how you have managed to make this a regular habit in your life?

LIBBIE: I've always taken Saturday mornings to catch up on the business section, read various financial magazines like *Kiplinger's* and update myself on the financial happenings of the week. I turn my cell phone off, my answering machine on, and ask my husband for no interruptions, unless it is totally necessary.

Once you put aside a certain amount of time every week, you know that's your time; don't allow yourself to be distracted. Whether it's learning real estate or financial planning, life is about forming new habits and being consistent with them. The confidence that comes from taking care of this aspect of your life radiates outward to everything you do.

VALERIE: What do you do differently than most people when recommending investments?

LIBBIE: As far as the actual investment side, I do things differently than what you read in books. To keep people on track, I start them investing right away. A lot of times you hear people say that you should save enough so that you have six months worth of income before you invest. Forget that. If you had to wait that long, most women would never be able to save that much money. What you could do from day one is pick one or two mutual funds that we recommend to beginners.

One kind is called a balanced mutual fund, which produces both growth and income, and the other kind is called a growth mutual fund. It takes anywhere between five hundred and a thousand dollars to begin investing in these funds. In our groups, we begin with these funds and have members contribute to their fund every week. We start working on that by educating and redirecting their spending philosophy. For example, if you go to Starbucks twice a week and spend $8 to $12, that's between $64 and $96 a month. Just think about what it would mean to put that money, which is between $768 and $1,152 a year, into a mutual fund? Instead of buying that coffee, write a check to your mutual fund.

VALERIE: Many women would have difficulty digesting this information and knowing how to put the first steps into action.

LIBBIE: Once you implement very specific steps to make financial decisions, it becomes easier. I look at it this way: If you're in your twenties, you need to put away 10 percent of your earnings, no matter how hard it is. And if you start in your thirties, it has to be 20 percent of your earnings, and if you start in your forties, it has to be 30 percent. The reason for this is that you don't have as much time to accumulate wealth because you're getting older.

VALERIE: How do you keep people motivated?

LIBBIE: To keep motivating people, we teach them Einstein's Rule of 72. Einstein's Rule of 72 tells you how quickly your money will double. It's an easy formula based on the interest you're earning. It's called the Rule of 72 because at 10 percent, money would double every 7.2 years. If you have ten thousand dollars in a savings account at a bank, earning you 2.5 percent, divide 2.5 percent into 72 to get 28.8 years to double your money. If you are thirty-five years old, with money earning 3 percent in the bank and doubling only every 24 years, you only have 1 double by age sixty. If you figure that inflation averages 3 percent you're just breaking even, if you don't figure the income taxes you paid on the 3 percent growth. If you're thirty-five and your money is growing at 12 percent, you have 6 doubles by age sixty. If you're fifty and your money is growing at 12 percent, you have 1.6 doubles left by age sixty. Eventually, this becomes an exercise that is fun for people. Teaching people how fast their money will grow based on the rate of interest they are earning allows them to make an educated decision. If you put your money in a mutual fund instead of a savings account, you will see it doubling, or growing, much faster. We do this in the classes that I teach, and women relate to it. They can constantly see results. The combination of trimming your lifestyle and maintaining it under strict control is not always easy. However, when you can see your investments starting to grow, it becomes easier and easier to save and will make you feel excited about doing it. The reality is you may need to sacrifice a little bit now to have what you want in the future.

VALERIE: I see a lot of new agents who make their first sale and then spend all of their money right away.

They end up creating a financial crisis for themselves. Knowing this, how would you better prepare them for their financial future?

LIBBIE: The biggest dilemma that everyone has, especially many younger women today, is living in the now versus the future. Not too long ago, I sold my business. This money is being used to endow YWCAs across the country to teach women financial literacy. We are using YWCAs because these organizations appeal to all women, all economic groups, all ethnic groups, and I'm team-teaching the classes there. A lot of the dilemmas that we've been discussing are about the present versus the future and how difficult it is to live in America today with all the media bombarding you daily on how to spend your money.

VALERIE: So how would you put this in perspective when women are contemplating their future?

LIBBIE: I think that the fear that every woman deals with, deep down, and it's something that I definitely stress, is that fear of being old, alone, and poor. I call it the Bag Lady Syndrome. The realities of living in the world today are complicated. You have to look over at Darfur or a place like that to contrast the kind of affluence and extravagance that we're exposed to in our country. We are now getting an inkling of those perspectives as we go forward daily, whether we are talking about the Iraq war or global warming. It's going to be tougher economically for Americans in the world and in our own country. And for women, I feel it will be the toughest. I believe women have always been three things: one, the great consumers; two, usually altruistic; and three, used to putting everyone—including their children and their parents—before themselves. It seems women have always put themselves last in line. Many hold on to the hope that someone will be there to take care of them, but that's not the reality anymore. No princes on white horses are in our future.

VALERIE: How can women really grasp this situation?

LIBBIE: This is something that has to be discussed and really emphasized. At this point in time, to take the independent roads we've taken as women we also have to accept that we've taken on total responsibility for ourselves, and there's nobody else who is going to do it. Our kids are not ever going to be able to take care of us, but that's what a lot of women think, and it's just not going to happen. So women have to get together in groups to start discussing these things. You also need to have the mentors and to talk to people who have gone the longer road. That way you will understand what sacrifices they've made so you can do the same to create financial security for your own life.

VALERIE: Would you say this could be an achievable goal for every woman? When would someone know that she has reached a financial goal?

LIBBIE: It is a goal for everyone. When you can earn as much as you need or want, that's when you know you've made it! For every $1 million that you can ever accumulate in your life, it will earn $50,000 a year for you if it's invested at 5 percent. That's why when you grow older, you should keep monitoring your lifestyle and monitoring your goals, so you will always know how much you'll need to accumulate. This can definitely be accomplished, because many women have done it. There are more and more women paying attention and taking charge of their lives.

VALERIE: How do women who are afraid to take the first step face this topic and discuss it openly?

LIBBIE: It can be frightening to a lot of people. A lot of women in my classes in the last twenty-five years pooled their money and bought a duplex together, and they started renting it out so that eventually they all had something. The idea of women working together and encouraging one another makes it so much easier, because they are moving together as a group. It then becomes easier to make the first step alone.

VALERIE: Are you doing anything in your current business life to make it easier for women simply to understand their finances?

LIBBIE: Yes. One of the things I'm working on is creating financial literacy groups across the country. I've put together and designed a kit, which I like to give to people as a means of coming together. The kits are made up of a little round box that you pull financial questions and topics out of for serious discussions with your friends.

VALERIE: Can you give us an example of what a woman in her late twenties or early thirties would have to invest now in order to be comfortable later in life?

LIBBIE: If we are talking about people living in an urban environment like New York or Los Angeles, I think for an older woman to be comfortable she needs an income of between $80,000 and $120,000. The reason I'm telling you this is because her health-care costs will be around 12 percent of what she has to spend per year. Health care is the biggie. So here's the strategy. I believe that Social Security will still be here, I don't think that's going to disappear. If someone is going to end up getting around $20,000 a year from Social Security, the rest of the money she has to accumulate by the earnings of her portfolio. The portfolio can be in bonds and stocks and real estate, rental properties. If she needs about $80,000, then she needs about $1.2 million in her portfolio, because $1.2 million earning 5 percent would give you $60,000 a year, and then you add your Social Security and then you have about $80,000. In the Midwest, a woman would need $50,000 to $80,000. The cost of living is considerably less.

VALERIE: Wow! That sounds like a lot of money to save for one woman. What is the one thing that you would like women to understand most about this process?

LIBBIE: The one thing I want them to realize is how much power they will have if they can accumulate some wealth so that they can not only take care of themselves and live the lifestyle they want but also understand that their money can bring social change in the world. Very small amounts of money can do that. Women don't realize just how much power they will have if they just focus on their finances. I believe this in my heart and I can see the evidence of it. I'm involved with an international group, it's called The Global Fund for Women, and we fund about $7 million worth of projects a year around the world. You cannot believe the change that two or three thousand dollars makes in some of these countries. Women can start a school, start a business, or clean up their water for around five thousand dollars. We can do it in our own country as well. Women can change the world.

Wealth Building Through Investment

Now that you better understand your net worth and ways to invest your hard-earned dollars, let us not forget that we are real estate agents. In so many areas of life, the best advice is, Do what you love! By loving what you do in life you are compelled to learn more and reach higher. Applied knowledge equates to growth and success. So, when you make an investment, invest in what you know.

You are learning real estate now. You can put your newfound skills to the test by investing in property on your own behalf. By loving what you do, you attain the skills and knowledge that not only serve your clients, but will serve you as well. Maybe you already have made your first investment in real estate, or perhaps you've bought and sold several properties. If you have experience in the area of investing in real estate it could be very helpful when advising clients. However, when it comes to your own personal investments, you may want to seek outside help yourself.

Many agents prefer to hire a fellow agent to represent them during the purchase or sale of a property. It really comes down to a personal choice as to how comfortable you feel about representing yourself. It's difficult to wear two or more hats at once, and sometimes the hardest thing is following your own advice. There may be some truth to the adage that "the person who represents himself has a fool for a client."

If you choose an agent in your office to assist you in your personal transactions, you need to listen when she gives you advice. Real estate is not only purchased as a means of shelter, but also as a solid investment. When interest rates are low, keeping money in the bank will not produce the same return as putting those same dollars into a real estate investment property. There are many times when the real estate market has outperformed the stock market. It has been statistically demonstrated that over time, there is no better investment than real estate.

Other People's Money

Clients will often look to you for advice about the investment value of a property, whether it's their intention to live in the home or to purchase it to generate income. If the property is being purchased as a family home, the first consideration is how the client's life would fit into that home. Only the client can answer that question. However, if the purchase is for investment purposes only, then we can offer the client an analysis of its potential to produce income. If you don't feel comfortable in this area of real estate, refer your client to an agent whom you trust who does sell investment property. It is an interesting area of our business, but it also requires knowledge in the areas of cap rates and gross multipliers that you'll need to communicate clearly to the client. Investment property is purchased more on a business level than on an emotional one. Again, if you don't feel comfortable selling this type of property, don't do it— refer the business to an agent who does specialize in investment properties. I have never focused on this area of the real estate business and have a limited knowledge of it. I believe in always doing my best for my clients and have chosen to familiarize myself with the process on a basic level and then refer my clients to agents who do specialize in the real estate investment field.

Property Development

I have represented many developers across the country. This is a specialty area in the real estate profession and not to be taken lightly. It involves a great deal of research and analysis of local real estate markets and trends. It takes coordination and cooperation on many levels for planning, pricing, and marketing, often years in advance of the grand opening date. The developer is putting his trust and money in you to know which units are the most likely to receive the highest prices when they are ready to sell. You have to know how to market and sell a project, when and where to offer incentives or concessions, and when to stay firm with the pricing. It's negotiation at a very high level and for very high stakes. Developers can make a lot of money or lose a bundle. To a great degree, the outcome could rest on your shoulders. Again, it's best to stick to what you know. This field is great if you have the knowledge and experience in it. If you don't and are interested to learn about this field of real estate, team up with an experienced agent who can teach you.

Investing Personally

As you take the time to budget your life, you will begin to accumulate small amounts of money that you've saved from your real estate transactions. At first you may be able to save one hundred dollars, then maybe five hundred dollars. These dollars will add up and will one day be the nest egg that you might use to purchase your personal residence.

Most people are much better off financially paying a mortgage every month to a bank rather than paying a monthly amount for rent. As a nation, we have many concerns about the economy and the price of basic needs. However, we also learn to live within our means, and without our means, and many people live above their means in order to have the opportunity to own their own home. When you own your own home there are financial considerations that can change. For instance, if you have a loan with a bank and want a lower payment, you'll probably get an adjustable loan whose interest rate will change with overall market conditions and is likely to go higher over time. If you are lucky enough to have a loan with a fixed rate of interest, your monthly payments will remain the same throughout the life of the loan. However, your income may change, as it does in real estate, and you could have a problem making your monthly payments. Either way, believe it or not, you have far more control over your life if you own your own home. Every choice we make every day, from the moment we get out of bed, has an element of risk to it. If you are renting your home, your landlord will certainly pass on the mortgage payment increases, property tax increases, insurance increases, and maintenance increases to you. This will be presented to you in the form of a rent increase. It is apparent that the majority of our population understands this fact in a very fundamental way. That's one of the major reasons why so many people choose to be homeowners.

Other significant advantages to owning a home are the tax deductions you are allowed and the chance to accumulate personal wealth through home ownership. You will build equity through a combination of making your monthly payments, reducing the amount that you owe the bank, and the market appreciation of your home over time. Usually, the longer you own your personal residence, the more it will increase in value. The real estate market will go up and down like any other market does, but it is proven over time to be the safest investment you can make. If you pay attention to the real estate market, watch your finances, and budget yourself, you will find your way toward building personal wealth.

Although most of the United States population is composed of homeowners, Americans are not good savers. As we've discussed before, having a reserve of money in any form is critical during periods of unemployment or for emergency needs. As a real estate professional, at times you will feel both unemployed and concerned about when you will receive your next commission check. It is crucial that you plan your life one step at a time and have someone to help guide you.

This book began in chapter 1 describing my living conditions. I was renting an apartment on the lower half of a two-unit building. As I became more aware, I began making lists of my expenses, including the repairs to my overheating Volkswagen. Every day I looked at real estate properties. I had an eye out for a place that I could afford to buy. One day I found a condominium on a street that was in a marginally good neighborhood. The area was near all of the clubs and bars, not exactly the family environment that I had envisioned. The building was dilapidated, but the new owner told me that he fully intended to fix up the property. When I entered the building, I actually felt scared. A guy was walking out of the lobby; he looked like he hadn't slept in months. He was pierced and tattooed everywhere that I could see, and I'm sure some places that I could not. To top it off, he had an orange Mohawk. This was a new experience for me. I was in a strange place in a neighborhood that I would have never frequented, and I was considering moving here with my precious baby. I was so close to turning back and bolting out the front door, but I didn't. Off the elevator I went, down this green shag carpeted hallway with fluorescent lighting. The man showing the building led me to a door at the end of the hall. I hadn't heard a word that he said while we were walking. All I could think about was what might await me on the other side of the door we were approaching. As the door swung open, I saw a stream of light coming through the windows and across the living room. The place was a wreck. I was relieved to find out that no one lived there. As I walked around it, I knew that it had potential. I could see and feel that this was a diamond in the rough. It had enough space for me and my daughter. If I fixed it up, I knew it would not only be beautiful, but the value of it would definitely go up! As we walked out of the condominium, my mind was racing. There were so many questions I needed to ask this man, to not only make a good deal but to feel comfortable that this would be a safe place to live. The walk back down the shag-carpeted hallway gave me a few minutes to contemplate my next move. Even though I saw a few more questionable characters as we walked, I decided to take the chance and buy the property. This was the first rung in the ladder of my home-ownership. It was a big step for me, but I knew that it was the right one. I had done my research. I had faith in my belief that the building would be upgraded and the occupants would become less alarming to me.

The building was eventually refurbished. The ugly duckling was transformed into a lovely place to call home. The occupants were no longer short-term renters and were now homeowners just like me. I remodeled our condominium as inexpensively as I could. It had a great look to it. Approximately eighteen months later I sold it for double what I paid and used that money to buy another condominium in a much better location.

As real estate professionals, we see many opportunities every day for both buyers and sellers. Often there will be times when clients won't see the value of the ugly duckling properties that you may see yourself. I traded up each of the four times I purchased a new personal residence until I bought the house of my dreams. Keep in mind that my ears and eyes were always open to opportunities for owning my own home. One of the things that I've always trusted is my intuition. How I feel about things is how I make decisions in my life. I'll bet you have all the tools you need to be a successful real estate professional and just don't realize it. Having personal wealth isn't as complicated as it seems. You have all of these abilities to make it happen, and I hope this book has given you the confidence to realize your dreams.

If we are divided all will fail.
If we are together nothing is impossible.

—WINSTON CHURCHILL

CHAPTER NINE

Lessons Learned

Your reputation, as you now realize, is crucial to your success in real estate and in life. The way you choose to conduct yourself will be reflected in your relationships. This holds true whether it is with a client, another agent, an assistant, or a partner. The people with whom you align yourself should share your values and project your business image. Choose carefully and wisely.

An assistant should have a presence, a style, and an energy level that are representative of you. A partner should provide the perfect balance to who you are and share your dreams of where you want to go. A partner will share the responsibility for the business and help do the work that you find difficult to do on your own. We have discussed many key ideas to becoming a successful agent. In this chapter we will discuss hiring an assistant and perhaps working with a partner.

How do you find out what works with other successful real estate agents? Well, I was lucky early in my career to join a mentoring group that offered me a great opportunity to grow personally and professionally. I participate in a mentoring group with nearly eighty agents working in markets across the United States and Canada. They are all top producers in their local areas, earning incomes between $1 million and $10 million a year. Yes, it can be done! They are ordinary people who share similar work ethics and values and who do extraordinary things on a daily basis by managing the heart and soul of people's lives.

When you have accumulated some experience as a real estate agent and arrived at the place where you are ready to jump to the next level of income and to invest in your own business, make sure that you are well prepared. You should begin to focus on where you're going and who is going with you. Will an assistant help you reach your goal? Will you partner up with another agent? Perhaps you will build your business slowly and over time assemble a professional team. Whichever style works for you, remember that real estate can provide unlimited financial opportunities to those who find the way to tap into them.

The national average income for real estate sales broker professionals is approximately $65,000 a year. This may be a significant income for you in the area where you work. However, consider this: with approximately two million active real estate licenses in the United States, there are more than five hundred thousand people in the real estate sales force in the United States who earn well over $1 million each year.

These top producers live and work in cities, small residential areas, and rural communities. We will discover why these individuals are so much more successful than other real estate agents and are able to generate the amazing commissions that they do.

Forming a Partnership

Partnering can be a wonderful opportunity. Two heads and two pairs of eyes can come in handy on those days when you're so busy multitasking that you feel you may lose the one head you have. When you need to be in two places at the same time, it's helpful to have another you.

Choosing a partner is very important. A partnership is like a marriage and has to be nurtured. It needs to be developed with care and strategic relationship building. It should be established based on a foundation of shared values and goals, mutual respect and trust, and a rock-solid commitment from both partners to each other and to the partnership. Specific partner roles, responsibilities, functions, and partnership priorities should be determined and agreed upon when the partnership is formed. It's important to be clear about these issues, establish a level of trust between you, and then not count every hour that each of you spends covering your area of responsibility. The important thing is that you and your partner are performing your agreed-upon roles.

BENEFITS OF PARTNERSHIP PRACTICE

You should each be aware of your strengths and weaknesses. Be honest with yourselves and with each other. You want to complement, not mirror each other. If you do share the same strengths and desires, then you may be fast friends but not necessarily best suited to be partners. You want to enhance the career and well-being of each other and the partnership. The greatest benefit of forming a partnership is that the sum of your combined efforts will be greater than what you could accomplish working on your own.

PICKING A PARTNER

I would suggest making a list of all of the aspects of the real estate business that we've discussed in previous chapters. It should include everything we've covered from marketing a property to marketing yourself to closing a transaction successfully when representing sellers or buyers. Separate the list into two columns of the business that you like and dislike. If you're not certain that you've included every element of the real estate business, ask your manager or training director to go over the lists with you. Be very honest with yourself. You should look for a partner who possesses the talent and desire to perform the functions you prefer not to do.

Certain personalities like to concentrate on and perform different aspects of the business. That is one of the components that makes for a wonderful working relationship. You and your partner will begin from the place of having something in common—you both love real estate. One of you may be more people oriented and enjoy meeting, greeting, and dealing with people more. The other partner may prefer to do paperwork, research, and analysis of systems and the marketplace. Perhaps one of you is more extroverted and the other more introverted and shy. Maybe one of you prefers working from the office and being a part of the office buzz, while the other person prefers to be out of the office, showing houses or meeting new prospects.

In a partnership, you can't both be the leader at the same time or you will be tripping over each other, duplicating work and confusing your clients. Instead of presenting a professional united front to other agents and prospects, you'll risk appearing incompetent. Who will be the point person for marketing? Who will be in charge of the mounds of paperwork in your business? Who will work certain hours in the office and be there to take the calls and questions? As you grow you have to be willing to put the partnership before your individual need for recognition. You must share the credit for every accomplishment with your partner and feel good that you have achieved your goals together. Maintain your individual talents within the framework of the partnership. Your mutual attitudes and thoughts must be a "WE," not an "I." Just like the relationships that you establish with your clients, treat your partnership with the trust and respect it deserves.

Hiring an Assistant

If you decide that sharing 50 percent of your business doesn't work for you, a better choice may be to hire an administrative assistant to help you with your business. The right time to make that decision will be based on your individual needs. You could do what I did and hire someone in anticipation of growing your real estate practice. For many agents, hiring an assistant before actually having the business in hand may feel like putting the cart before the horse. It is up to you to make the determination of how much business you are personally willing to handle and when you'll need to hire someone to help you. Are you able to cover the sales, marketing, and administration of your business? Do you feel as though you are spread too thin? At some point you will likely need some sort of support for the things that need to be accomplished on a daily basis. In real estate, we have an expression that says, "If you don't have an assistant, you are the assistant." You will easily find out how true this is if you are doing everything in your real estate practice yourself.

Having an administrative assistant who runs your office and handles the phones and paperwork can be invaluable. Not only will you have relief from the piles of administrative work, but the time savings will enable you to better balance your professional and personal life and will improve customer service for your clients. We all struggle with the element of time in our lives. We always seem to be looking for more of it. So why not leverage your time by hiring someone to do the things you don't want to do?

When hiring your first assistant, you need to consider whether you need full-time or part-time help. If your business is growing slowly, perhaps hiring a part-time assistant is more appropriate. You could begin by sharing the cost of the salary with another agent. This will not mean you are partners, only sharing someone to help both of you with your respective real estate practices.

If your business is growing rapidly, then you may choose to hire a full-time assistant. It would be best to hire someone who has real estate experience. In any event, you will need to make a comprehensive list of duties you expect your assistant to perform. You should check with local real estate board rules to know what duties require an assistant to have a real estate license. This may differ from state to state.

Now the question is whom to hire. Someone who is like you? Someone with whom you instantly form a bond? Should you consider someone who may have talents and excel in areas you don't? Hiring the right person for the right fit is tricky. You have to match your working style and assess the capabilities of the assistant to complete the required work. Take your time when interviewing people and be sure you feel comfortable with them. Ask about their work experience, check their references, and take note of how long they have stayed at their last place of employment. People who move around professionally will be a problem if you need to rely on them. They may suddenly give you notice that they've found another job. Once you do find someone, hire him and invest your time in training him in the ways you want things done.

I have had my share of employment blunders, picking the wrong people for various positions. Although I have often had assistants who worked with me for years, eventually it is time for everyone to have a change. Hiring new people can also bring about fresh ideas and new positive attitudes.

Early on I worked in a company where there was a seasoned agent who was so savvy and organized that I was certain that she had her eyes on everything. It appeared she felt the same way, so she began to let down her guard with her staff and people in the office. She had an assistant who, unbeknownst to her, had run into financial difficulties. Since he did not have access to her financial accounts, he did the next best thing and slowly began endearing himself to her client list to gain their confidence. He then proceeded to tell these clients that the agent he was working for was too busy to work with them and that she had asked him to see to their needs. He was so believable that many clients never questioned his honesty. After all, they had actually known him for many years as the agent's personal assistant. By the time the agent was aware of the situation, the assistant had sold three houses worth more than $1 million each without the agent's knowledge or consent. Once the agent realized the situation, it took a lot of time and energy for her to repair the damage done by her desperate assistant. Professionally she took the high road and never uttered a bad word about him in the real estate community. She didn't have to; as seasoned agents know, there are no secrets in real estate. Good, bad, or indifferent, information travels quickly, whether you want it to or not. She did end up firing that assistant and then went immediately to work repairing the damage that he had caused to her business.

The lesson is to pay attention to what is going on around you, especially in your business. We get so blinded by our own busy world that we get caught up in situations we could have prevented.

Assistants, as I've said, can be invaluable for helping you grow your business. They can be in the office when you are door knocking or while you're in the office cold calling. They can field calls and questions from other agents about properties, returning calls that you really don't need to return personally. Assistants with real estate experience can help you with Sunday open houses, buyer's showings, and preparing materials for listing appointments. I think you'll find that the freedom gained by employing a personal assistant will not only help grow your business but will give you the time to appreciate the life you work so hard to create.

GOING VIRTUAL

As you now know, finding the right assistants requires a significant amount of time and effort. It can make you wonder if there isn't an easier way. The traditional way many agents go about hiring assistants is sometimes by placing an ad in the local paper or advertising by word of mouth. However, there are many ways to access qualified people through technology. Websites like Craigslist or Monster.com can easily assist you. But what if you don't need someone everyday and would like to only hire someone for specific projects? These positions are called "virtual assistants." They usually work from their homes, which can be anywhere in the world, and they get paid only when completing the project they were hired to do. To learn more about virtual assistants, I have interviewed Michael Russer. Also known as Mr. Internet, Michael is a renowned international speaker, author, and columnist. He specializes in helping independent professionals and businesses of all types incorporate innovative productivity strategies to achieve a higher level of personal and career fulfillment. Michael owns several companies and has been blissfully "employee free" for more than thirteen years, but he has many incredibly talented people all around the world who conduct business for him, most of whom he has never met face to face.

VALERIE: Michael, can you explain to us what virtual outsourcing is and its benefits to those in real estate?

MICHAEL: The process of outsourcing means delegating various job functions so that they do not involve the real estate agent's time. The agent hires virtual assistants or specialists who are masters in their area of expertise.

There are many benefits to hiring a virtual assistant. First, it frees you up to do what you do best—list, sell, and negotiate. A virtual assistant helps you with your business in the same way that a regular assistant would, except all the work is done over the Internet, e-mail, and fax. These assistants don't require space, cost less, and can offer a quicker turnaround on their work.

VALERIE: So when agents try to do everything themselves, does it keep them in their office too much of the time?

MICHAEL: Absolutely. When agents try to do everything themselves, it takes them away from the action and keeps them in their office. It's no secret that salespeople are not great at managing other people. When they are interviewing potential employees, they gravitate toward people like themselves. In reality, the best personality to go with is not one that is just like yours. The best employees may not have vivacious personalities yet they may be excellent at what they do. People in sales hire people for the wrong reasons and end up spending all their time trying to motivate them.

VALERIE: So, Michael, how would you hire assistants in nontraditional ways?

MICHAEL: Just think about it. What if you didn't have to hire a traditional staff? What if you were able to hire an assistant not by making a judgment call but instead hired them based on the individual's ability, with no fear of having a personality conflict? For example, a virtual assistant who specializes in coordinating and marketing your listings will provide you with a competitive advantage and help you make more money and allow you more time to meet your client's needs.

VALERIE: You mentioned that virtual assistants have specialties. Can you tell us what those specialties are and how they would be useful to a new agent?

MICHAEL: There are three types of virtual assistants that a new agent might consider. The first would be a transaction coordinator. They handle and track all the paperwork, making sure that all deadlines are met. Next there is the listing marketing coordinator, who handles all the aspects of marketing a new listing and keeping the seller informed through weekly progress reports. Lastly is the drip marketing specialist, who is in charge of sending out postcards and mailings. Most agents get bogged down and can't keep up with their sphere of influence. Studies show that 83 percent of buyers and sellers are pleased with their agent and would use the same agent in future transactions. Yet 11 percent don't use their agent again because that agent didn't maintain the relationship.

Let's say you're a new agent and you get five new listings. That's pretty exciting. Yet fifteen minutes later, when you start to think about all the work that goes into managing those listings, you're not feeling so excited. However, when you are working with a virtual marketing coordinator, they create customized documents, manage a website with multiple photos with links to showing-request forms, disclosures, flyers, preinspection reports, and any other pertinent information. They create virtual tours and a PowerPoint marketing presentation for you to use during your initial meeting with prospects that outlines all the marketing activities you will provide. The virtual assistant also provides them with a weekly report based on all the information received on the projects from various sites like Realtor.com, Google Local, and Craigslist.org.

Imagine sitting down as a new agent and presenting this to your potential prospect. Utilizing this technology gives you a great advantage over more experienced agents who have been in the business longer but who do everything themselves. The added bonus is that you, the agent, only pay the listing marketing coordinator on a per project basis for each listing.

VALERIE: It's amazing just how much a virtual assistant can do. My second assistant in real estate moved to a rural part of Oregon. However, she was able to continue working for me as a virtual assistant. Since I had an established working relationship with her, there was no interviewing involved. Can you share with us how to go about finding an online virtual specialist and how the interview process goes?

MICHAEL: There are websites that specialize in real estate–specific specialists: www.virtualassistants.com, www.revanetwork.com, and www.virtualassistants jobs.com.

You can also hire virtual consultants to handle specific projects like marketing. These online consultants bid against one another for the job. They don't know who you are, but you know who they are and can view samples of their work. One of the benefits is that you can retain them for a project without having them work for you as full-time staff. You can find these services at www.elance.com, www.guru.com, and www.ifreelance.com.

VALERIE: Michael, how do you stay professional and exercise professional due diligence when conducting online interviews?

MICHAEL: I really feel that all communications should be done by e-mail because you want to hire based on ability and not by the charm on the other end of the phone line. Follow up on the references given to you.

VALERIE: What are the most important questions when qualifying a virtual assistant?

MICHAEL: The five most important questions to ask when interviewing a virtual assistant are:

1. Why are you the best specialist out there to supply the work I need done?

2. What assurances can you give me that you aren't taking on more work than you can handle?

3. How do I know my work won't fall through the cracks if something happens to you?

4. Ask for the names of three to five current clients that she has been working with for at least six months. Make sure the references you check are for the same kind of job you need done.

5. Ask for a list of three people who were clients whom they are no longer working with. You want to know why.

A professional virtual assistant will know how to answer these questions. If you sense any stumbling or read any vague answers, don't walk—run for the hills.

VALERIE: An agent interviewing virtual assistants may get a sense of who they are, but how do the virtual assistants get a sense of the agent?

MICHAEL: Good question. Keep in mind that a good virtual assistant will be interviewing you as well. A good virtual assistant never wants to see the following in an agent:

1. A boss/employee relationship. There is no hierarchy in this relationship. It is two businesses working together for the betterment of both.

2. Arrogance.

3. An agent who is unclear.

4. An agent who lives constantly in the urgent.

A virtual assistant's job is to get things done in a timely fashion so that the urgency fire doesn't happen.

Look at your business as a business. Systematically and incrementally bring on support as your business grows.

VALERIE: What is the most important advice you would give to agents?

MICHAEL: First, specialize! Do not make the mistake of trying to be everything to everybody. If you specialize in being a listing agent, then make it your business to know everything there is to know about listings. Keep records and document your business so that you have a business to sell when you want to retire.

I was speaking in Canada when I heard the story of a young man who went into real estate. He didn't know anything about the business, but he was intuitive enough to know that he needed to specialize. He chose to specialize in condos. He taught himself everything there was to know about buying, selling, condo fees, negotiating this market, and all other pertinent information. Two years later he had made himself a millionaire and is referred to as the "Condo King." Now if you wanted to buy a condo in his market, who would you go to? Someone who specialized in several different markets or the Condo King?

VALERIE: So would you advise a new agent to learn the most that he can about niches in his market areas?

MICHAEL: Yes I would. Start with one thing that could be a niche market. After you become an expert in that field, then decide whether or not to take on other areas. Make sure that you choose a specialty that makes you feel most fulfilled as a human being. If a certain area of real estate is to be your specialty, you have to enjoy it. Own the expertise that you develop, and understand the personalities exclusive to that market. Strive to own that specialty.

VALERIE: What other advice do you have?

MICHAEL: My second piece of advice is to set up your business as a business. What is my highest value? Anytime you do anything outside your core competency—listing, selling, or negotiating—you are paying top dollar for amateur results. Or worse, you risk that the task at hand will not get done or will fall through the cracks. As a new agent, start by hiring the critical components, like a transaction coordinator. This allows you to direct all your energy to building your business and developing your core competency skills. While some people are natural salespeople, many aren't. Delegating responsibilities to your virtual assistants allows you to put your time into you and your abilities. Get coaching on the fundamentals of sales and people skills.

My last piece of advice is to be aware of how very easy it is to be owned by this business. For most of us, the issue of survival has been licked. Our time is now spent in the pursuit of some level of affluence and comfort while working too hard to enjoy it. It's important to structure your business around your life.

VALERIE: Could you give me a real life example?

MICHAEL: Several years ago I was speaking in Texas. There were two elderly ladies who were sitting in the front row. During the break we started talking. They looked like average elderly women in their sixties. There was nothing unusual about them aside from the twinkle in their eyes and their youthful spirit. They shared with me the tales of their latest trip to New Zealand, where they tried bungee jumping! Then they went on to share how they were getting ready to visit Antarctica. "Antarctica!" I said. "Why there?" "It's the only continent we never visited before," one lady responded. I asked them how they could afford to take so much time off. Very matter-of-factly they said that they always plan their business around their life, not the other way around. Decide what you need for you.

VALERIE: How do you structure your busy professional life and yet spend time with your family?

MICHAEL: I can only tell you that it's important to schedule dates that are just for you and your family. You have to have time off to smell the roses. Your sense of self-worth cannot be wrapped up in your career. I was speaking in Michigan when a woman raised her hand. I didn't know it at the time, but she was the number two agent in the state. She said that she only slept two to three hours a night. Can you imagine? This woman was doing every part of her business herself, which left her no time to sleep. Not only had the joy gone out of her life, but she was putting her health at risk. I told her I would help her change her life, but she didn't see how I could. I taught her about outsourcing and having a virtual assistant. She e-mailed me later, thanking me; she was finally getting a full night's sleep and was much happier and healthier.

Team Building

You will have a varied collection of real estate partners along the way in building your business. They will be your team. In the beginning of your career, you will interact with and rely upon your fellow agents and staff members in the brokerage office. They will assist you in marketing yourself and closing your sales. They will be your first team members.

As you become more successful, you will undoubtedly

consider building a team of your own. A fully assembled team might include the following members:

1. Personal assistant

2. Call and showing assistant

3. Office administrator

4. Transaction coordinator

5. Director of sales

6. Buyer's agents

7. Marketing coordinator

Building a team will give you a foundation from which to conduct your business. So do your research. Make sure that you know what you really need to know to grow your business, and don't add too many people to your team in the beginning stages. Take your time to see how each team member performs her position. Once you see that everyone is working well together, the sky's the limit!

We begin our careers as independent sales agents. As we grow our business, we find it necessary to hire others to help manage what we've created. Usually, we have no formal skills at knowing whom to hire and under what terms and conditions to employ them. True to our independent contractor nature, we often figure out things as we go along in the realm of employment and business management.

I had no personal experience whatsoever employing staff

when I hired my first assistant. Fortunately, she was open to the experience of working with me even though I really had no specific job description for her position. As I mentioned in chapter 4, I simply gave her a list of the things that I didn't want to do myself. We've stayed in touch, and to this day, she and I laugh about that experience. My second assistant was amazing. She was far smarter than I in administrative tasks. I was so grateful for her knowledge. I listened to and learned from her. She eventually moved to another state, but she remains my assistant in a different way. She and I now have a virtual working relationship. We don't see each other, but we do work on projects together. As you've read in Michael Russer's interview, in today's technological world, the possibilities for new kinds of business relationships are endless.

As my business grew, I felt that I needed specific staff in different areas to accomplish my goals. One thing I knew for sure was that time was my most precious commodity. I needed more of it to work with potential clients and to bring in more business.

It took five or six years of choosing the wrong people, with all of the accompanying consequences, before I found the right people. During this time, I learned a lot about my administrative skills and the way I wanted my business to operate.

When I started, I thought that I gave out enough information to complete the tasks properly and in a timely fashion. After all, my initiation had been, "Here's your desk, and here's your empty Rolodex. Now, get to work." I was so relieved to have people doing things for me. I could now focus all of my energy on selling properties, and I did not pay a lot of attention to running my office. There was a time when I felt very complacent and comfortable with my administrative staff, with whom I'd worked for years, and I stopped being attentive to the internal workings of my business. At one point, I found that the infrastructure of my office had begun to unravel and discovered there were a number of disgruntled people who pretended to be a happy cohesive team. After trying to work through some of their issues, I made the necessary changes and learned to never assume or take things for granted ever again. Never let go of your business. If you hire the right staff, you will be able to step away, but never abandon what you've created.

Over the years, I have worked with many personalities. Everyone takes in information differently, and it's important to communicate clearly with each team member. Real estate is a people-oriented business. Whether you have employees, partners, or clients, we need to work together to further all of our careers and goals.

When things are going well, don't forget about the salaries and bonuses you need to include in your budget. All of your team's income depends on what you're bringing in at the end of the day. Your sales may not have increased at the same pace as your team-building efforts. Your expenses may have doubled to cover your team's salary requirements, and this increase might keep you from sleeping at night.

About ten years into my real estate career, I faced exactly this situation. I felt like I was driving the bus for a staff of four and others whom I was supporting financially. I faced an incredible amount of pressure to find a way to increase my business and leverage my time. There were no more hours in a day. My staff seemed busy. I couldn't do more. So I reached out to people who could. I built a sales team. A sales team is very different from a sales staff. I knew that most people in sales were like me and didn't like doing administrative tasks.

I looked for talented new agents who wanted to work with me. I decided to offer administrative support for agents, which they could never afford on their own. I would agree to mentor them, to make myself available, and to share my knowledge, and in return we shared commissions as they were earned. I knew that I could build an incredible team of professional agents, and I understood the value of our combined strength.

At this time in my business I have a wonderful group of eight junior agents working with me. I also have an administrative staff of five very talented people. We call my sales group "buyer's agents," because when starting out in real estate you work more with buyers. They have the opportunity to meet many more buyers than they would from calling their database by sitting the Sunday open houses that I provide to them. Each week we meet as a group on Tuesday afternoon to review their Sunday activities, good buys, and property activities and to discuss their questions and concerns. These are very productive meetings where we share the previous week's experiences and everyone learns from one another.

There are assorted discussions about handling problems

with people they meet, the rise and fall of property values, contract questions, or even just venting frustrations. Many times the buyer's agents are experiencing new territory. Having people hang up or yell at you when you're trying to help them can be hard to swallow. Sometimes it helps them to better understand their experience when I have them role-play the situation with me. These exercises give them insight into how they could react and perhaps handle the situation differently.

There are other days when the buyer's agents meet together to review their systems and goals as a team. How many calls are they going to make where they actually speak to someone? How many buyer's appointments ("buyer's consults") did they get out of their Sunday open house? How many appointments can they make to get prospects out to look at homes? In addition, there are mandatory meetings with vendors, where they learn about title, escrow, inspections, and government requirements. These systems keep them accountable and heading down a productive path.

One thing I try to do each day when I arrive at the office is to go to the desk of each of my administrative staff, smile, and ask them how they are, whether there is anything I need to know, and whether there is anything that they need from me. This always sets up an open, friendly environment where everyone feels valued. Each member of my administrative staff has his or her own set hours to be in the office. As the day winds down, and as each person leaves, I always thank them for a job well done. Who said independent contractors can't manage people?

Designing Your Life

Design your life and then find the job.

–LOU TICE

This quote by Lou Tice says it all. As the expression goes, "Necessity is the mother of invention." I've reinvented myself numerous times. I learned how to design my life through trial and error. Life can often be a ride in a bumper car. Bumping into situations along my path, I have taken with me what I wanted and left the rest behind.

This is how I designed my life and found the career that I love. The following are true stories of people in real estate. As you will see, these people have come from various backgrounds. They too bumped into real estate and built a successful career.

Along the way, while building my business, I learned and experienced things about people and the world in which we live. The results of my life have certainly been created by my own hand. At times I've wondered if the girl in the apartment with the baby, scared about what she would do next in life, could meet the executive in the office today, what would they have said to each other?

BETTY–CALIFORNIA

I was born one of eight on a cotton farm in Alabama. At fifteen, my family piled everything we owned on top of the car and we drove to the San Joaquin Valley in California, where we lived as migrant workers. I married my high school sweet-heart at seventeen years old. Unfortunately, I wasn't ready for marriage, and less than a year later, single again, I moved to the big city of Los Angeles.

Luckily, I found work right away. I worked in various studios as a producer's assistant and attended UCLA at night. I eventually landed a job as Johnny Carson's personal assistant. I met and married my second husband and had a beautiful baby boy. When my son was six years old, my husband and I separated. I had been a stay-at-home wife and mother and suddenly needed to support myself and my son. I obtained my real estate license in 1976.

With no instruction, I was simply a natural at the business of representing clients buying or selling real estate. My self-esteem soared as I helped my friends and the clients they referred to me find a house or sell a house. It was immensely exciting work to me, and I couldn't get enough of it. I couldn't sleep, and I couldn't rest, because I was on fire with the joy this business gave me. Frankly, it is still that way for me.

ALISON–CALIFORNIA

I was born on a rural New Hampshire farm in a town without a traffic light. I grew up surrounded by the beauty of nature and consequently developed a strong passion for the environment. I received my degree in biology and environmental science from Kenyon College in rural Ohio. I never expected to live in Los Angeles or sell multimillion dollar homes by the beach, but here I am.

When I became a Realtor I did not want to sacrifice any of my values. If I was going to be a Realtor then I wanted to be an honest, genuine, and "green" Realtor. I joined a paper-less office, and they provided me with the technology and training to complete my clients' transactions entirely on tablet computer. As a new agent I was told that in order to succeed I needed to send mailings to my client database. This presented me with a dilemma; I did not want to be another person cutting down trees only for my letters to end up in the junk-mail pile. My solution was to find environmentally friendly printers to produce my mailers.

Not only am I a new agent, but at twenty-four years old I am considered fairly young for this type of business. More than once I have had clients look at me with a con-fused/concerned expression and ask, "How old are you?" It's true that I'm young, and to be honest, I don't think I had ever felt the weight of real responsibility before. All of a sudden I was responsible for the life savings, dreams, and futures of families. It feels so wonderful to be part of making someone's dreams come true. Some clients are so grateful that I almost feel unworthy; after all, I'm just doing my job. To be present at that moment and to be able to share the happiness someone feels when they achieve their first home is fantastic. These are moments I will always remember and the reason I am a Realtor.

KRIS—CALIFORNIA

I grew up in Dearborn, Michigan, and became a professional dancer at sixteen years old. Two years later, right after high school graduation, I caught a ride with a friend to New York City to be a professional dancer. I danced as a Rockette at Radio City Music Hall.

The Rockette organization asked me, along with a few other dancers, to accompany them to Los Angeles. I decided that I liked it there and made it home. I took all kinds of jobs dancing. At one point I decided that I'd had enough and wanted to do something else.

Some friends suggested that I look into getting a real estate license. So I went back to waiting tables at night, which I hadn't done since my early days in New York, and went to real estate school during the day. I passed the exam and interviewed with offices. The first manager with whom I spoke told me that she wouldn't hire me unless I quit my job waiting tables. I couldn't afford to do that. She wished me well and sent me on my way. I didn't appreciate her attitude because it made me feel like she didn't believe in me. Maybe in retrospect she made me try even harder.

The next manager hired me, and my first six months were so productive, I did quit my night job. I had no idea that the market would suddenly collapse. For the next two years I struggled to pay my rent, pay my real estate fees, make my car payment, and eat. My credit card balances were at their limits.

I started to temp at television studios. I never gave up wanting to be in real estate. I didn't have any listings, so any opportunity that was offered to sit another agent's Sunday open house, I took. One day, the real estate office manager received a call from a major corporate client who needed an agent to market and sell property that had fallen into foreclosure. I was the first person he saw and I jumped at the chance.

I had no idea what the work would entail, no idea of the hours, but I didn't care. My first full year working for this account, I sold 157 properties. I was working sixteen-hour days, seven days a week and was so grateful. I learned so much and was more than happy to share my knowledge with other agents.

I love my work and the whole real estate process. I never forgot the agents who helped me. I want to honor them by helping other agents. I have never forgotten my early days. I will always take special care of the new agents coming into the business. Life is full of wonderful moments.

A Call

I was in my office one day when I received a call from a woman who said she worked on the police force in another city. The conversation went something like this:

CALLER: I'm a black policewoman, and I've been on the police force for thirteen years. I'm a divorced single mother and the sole supporter of two children under the age of twelve. I've been struggling financially and can barely make ends meet. I've always wanted to go into real estate and didn't know what to do next. What would you suggest should be my first step?

VALERIE: First you need to get some help taking care of your children at night so you can take classes and get your real estate license. I used to share babysitting with a neighbor. Do you have relatives or neighbors who can help you watch your children?

CALLER: I'll try and figure that out. Thank you.

VALERIE: Let me know how you do. I'll be rooting for you.

A few months later, she called me back.

VALERIE: So, how's it going?

CALLER: I found someone to help with my children and did exactly what you suggested. I just passed my real estate exam and will have my license any day. I still can't afford to quit my day job. What do you suggest I do next?

VALERIE: Figure out what days you need to work in your present job. Then find a real estate office and see how you can work with them. Ask if there is an agent you can work alongside or shadow part time. This will give you the opportunity to learn more. Arrange for child care on those days so you'll have the time to get a feel for whether you really like real estate. Let me know what happens.

A short time later:

> **CALLER:** I'm so excited. I just wanted you to know that
> I resigned from the police force. I just sold my second
> house. I have made more money so far this year than
> I can ever remember. Thank you!

I have shared my voice through this book, and I am truly grateful to you for taking the time to read it. As with most things, there is no right or wrong way in life, just the journey of our choices. I wanted to be successful. Desiring success is a very powerful step to take along the road to achieving it. I am still on my journey. There is so much to do in our lives! To live the new possibilities of your imagination is exciting. The possibilities and choices are endless. Just as the sky and the ocean meet in an infinite way, so go your possibilities! All you need is the heart and desire to make your own visions come true.

Something to remember if you are considering the real estate profession as a career is that it is one of the few fields with absolutely no discrimination. You can be any age when you start, be any race, have almost any background, speak any language, or have any accent. What you need is a smile on your face, a deep desire, and the heart to go out and get it.

You only have one life to live. Try something new. Dare to dream. Go and live your life OUT LOUD! I urge you to turn all of your energy and attention now to what you know you deserve. Pursue your dreams with a sense of determination, as fast as you can. You will have challenges navigating certain moments in your life. We all do. Just think of how over the moon you will be once you get where you have always wanted to go!

If you shoot for the moon and miss, remember, you are still among the stars.

We fail forward to success.

–MARY KAY

Acknowledgments

I am sure you have heard the African proverb, "It takes a village to raise a child." Admittedly it was challenging for me to write things about my personal and professional life. It took a lot of reflection for me to express myself in my own words. Although cathartic and unimaginably fulfilling in the end, it was a daunting task to undertake. As the African proverb so clearly illustrates, it takes the support of others to make things happen—including raising a child. We need to help one another be the best we can be.

I could never have written this book without the support of some very important people in my life.

First of all, my respect and deep appreciation for Debra Ziven, my real estate colleague and friend. Debra and I both have full-time real estate businesses we operate during the day. Nearly every night we collaborated on this book, often laughing at many of the stories I was telling in these pages. Debra is centered, talented, and very wise.

I have profound respect and gratitude for my very good friend Nancy Hutson Perlman. Her insights and ability to see things clearly when I couldn't was immeasurably important to me. Nancy was always there to answer my questions *and* my calls, day or night. Nancy and I have been friends so long she has lived through many of the stories you read about in this book.

And then there is my BFF Kathy Villa, who also happens to be my real estate colleague. Kathy and I still speak a minimum of three times a day. Her relentless support and honest feedback have been a great source of strength for me. She has had difficult personal challenges, yet she is probably the happiest person you will ever meet.

You will have read about my friend Kathleen Stewart, the very talented interior designer. As you saw, we have experienced so much life together and have come through it laughing. She always told me I was lucky to have her because she did all the worrying. She was Ethel and I was Lucy. All these years that has stuck—we will forever be Ethel and Lucy.

These incredible women are all a part of my "village." It is time for you to find yours and treasure every minute of those relationships.

Special Thanks

The initial opportunity to write this book began when my friend Byron Allen, CEO of Entertainment Studios Inc., asked me several years ago if I would do an interview for a television show, *Every Woman*. This show was about inspiring women who made a difference in their own lives and the lives of other people. It was this show that my editor, Johanna Castillo of Atria Books, saw, and it prompted her to call me to see if I would be interested in writing a book. True to my nature, although I had no idea of how to write a book, I said yes. So here we are. My sincere thank you to these people for believing in me.

The poem "After a While" by Veronica A. Shoffstall was given to me by my mother when I was pregnant with my daughter. I've reread it many times over the years. Thank you, Mom.

Recommended Reading

These are suggested readings that the author found helpful at various stages. Please seek your own professional advice, as well.

Miscellaneous

Lois P. Frankel, Ph.D., *Nice Girls Don't Get the Corner Office*

Barbara Corcoran, *Use What You've Got & Other Business Methods I Learned from My Mom*

Kim Lavine, *Mommy Millionaire*

Yasmin Davidds, *Take Back Your Power*

Dr. Rachael Heller and Dr. Richard Heller, *Healthy Selfishness*

Susan Nolen-Hoeksema, Ph.D., *Women Who Think Too Much*

George Mair, *A Life With Purpose*

Gary Zukav, *The Seat of the Soul*

Fran Hewitt and Les Hewitt, *The Power of Focus for Women*

Chris Gardner with Quincy Troupe, *The Pursuit of Happyness*

Susan Jeffers, Ph.D., *Feel the Fear . . . and Do It Anyway*

Anthony Robbins, *Unlimited Power*

David R. Hawkins M.D., Ph.D., *Power vs. Force*

Juliet Nierenberg and Irene S. Ross, *Negotiate for Success*

Keith Harrell, *Attitude Is Everything*

David Niven, Ph.D., *The 100 Simple Secrets of Successful People*

Financial

Susan Reynolds and Robert Bexton, CFA, *The Everything Guide To Personal Finance for Single Mothers*

James O. Parker, *The Weekend Real Estate Investor*

Eric Tyson and Robert S. Griswold, *Real Estate Investing for Dummies*

Wallace D. Wattles, *The Science of Getting Rich*

Lois P. Frankel, Ph.D., *Nice Girls Don't Get Rich*

Michael Gerber, *E-Myth*

Robert T. Kiyosaki, *Rich Dad, Poor Dad*

Gary W. Carter, *J.K. Lasser's Taxes Made Easy for Your Home-Based Business*

Gwendalyn Beck, *Flirting with Finance*

Belief Systems

Paula Muran, *Codes Of Light: The Power of Our Beliefs and a Revolutionary System To Heal Them*

Vera A. Gonzales, *Your Power Belief System: Change Your Life One Belief at a Time*

Thad B. Green and Merwyn Hayes, *The Belief System: The Secret To Motivation and Improved Performance*

Lane Jennings, *A House Divided: Six Belief Systems Struggling for the American Soul*

Esther and Jerry Hicks, *Ask and It Is Given*

Rhonda Byrne, *The Secret*

Paul Arden, *It's Not How Good You Are, It's How Good You Want To Be*

Thinking Big

David J. Schwartz, Ph.D., *The Magic of Thinking Big*

Ben Carson, M.D., with Cecil Murphey, *Think Big: Unleashing Your Potential for Excellence*

Les Brown, *Live Your Dreams*

Erika Welz Prafder with Carole Sovocool, *Keep Your Paycheck, Live Your Passion*

Leadership

Stephen R. Covey, *Principle-Centered Leadership*

Larry Holman and Bunny Holman, *Turning Dreams into Success: Lessons in Leadership from the Ground Up*

John C. Maxwell, *The 21 Irrefutable Laws of Leadership*

John C. Maxwell, *Leadership Promises for Every Day*

Jon P. Howell and Dan L. Costley, *Understanding Behaviors for Effective Leadership*

Marshall Loeb and Stephen Kindel, *Leadership for Dummies*

Anthony Robbins, *Awaken the Giant Within*

James Kouzes and Barry Z. Posner, *The Leadership Challenge*

Real Estate

Steve Kantor, *Billion Dollar Agent — Lessons Learned*

Gary Keller, Dave Jenks, and Jay Papasan, *The Millionaire Real Estate Agent*

Tom Hopkins, *Selling for Dummies*

Marilyn Sullivan, *The Complete Idiot's Guide to Success as a Real Estate Agent*

Tom Hopkins, *How to Master the Art of Listing and Selling Real Estate*

Stuart Leland Rider, *Millionaire Homeowner*

Ilyce R. Glink, *100 Questions Every First Time Home Buyer Should Ask*

Team

Patrick Lencioni, *The Five Dysfunctions of a Team*

Website References

REAL ESTATE:

www.ValerieFitzgerald.com

www.LosAngelesRealEstateTalk.com (blog)

www.Realtor.org

www.Realtor.com

www.mls.com

www.homes.com

www.homesadvisor.com

www.numberexpert.com

www.workingwomentoday.com

COACHING

www.coachken.com

www.ckginternational.com

www.pacificinstitute.com

www.valeriefitzgeraldmentoring.com

TRACKING EXPENSES

www.Quicken.com

www.QuickBooks.com

FINANCIAL

www.Kiplinger.com

www.money.com

www.moneyfool.com

www.globalfundforwomen.org

www.wsj.com

CONTACT AND SOFTWARE PLANNERS

www.act.com

www.topproducer.com

www.palm.com

www.franklincovey.com

www.ataglance.com

www.dayrunner.com

GOING VIRTUAL

www.virtualassistants.com

www.revanetwork.org

www.virtualassistantjobs.com

www.elance.com

www.guru.com

www.ifreelance.com

STRESS

www.lhj.com/relax